Imperialism and

and

INDIANA UNIVERSITY PRESS

BERNARD S. MORRIS

Revolution

An Essay for Radicals

BLOOMINGTON & LONDON

Published in Canada by Fitzhenry &
Whiteside Limited, Don Mills, Ontario
Library of Congress catalog card number: 73–81164
ISBN: 0–253–32920–5 cl. 0–253–20170–5 pa.
Manufactured in the United States of America

Contents

Acknowledgments

To my good friends John H. Kautsky and Samuel Sharp
for their critical reading of the manuscript.

To Indiana University's Russian and East European Institute for summer grants.

For the Senior Fulbright-Hays Scholar award, 1972–73,
which enabled me to complete the manuscript in Yugo-
slavia.

In many respects this book is addressed to concerns voiced
by my students in the late 1960's; I acknowledge the stimu-
lation.

Preface

As the magnitude of the ruin visited on Indochina increased, destroying any semblance of proportion between means and ends of policy, the inadequacy of "containment" as a rational explanation of United States foreign policy became increasingly apparent. The American war on Vietnam, initially viewed as the logical extension of a policy devised after World War II to contain putative Communist expansion into western and southern Europe, appeared to have developed into an aberrational anti-Communism. In casting about for a theoretical framework adequate to explain U.S. foreign policy in the 1960's, commentators turned to the time-honored idea of imperialism. What had been stock in trade for Marxists became part of the everyday vocabulary of liberal and conservative writers. Most, but not all, used the idea of imperialism as a wedge for a critical analysis of American policy; a few viewed it rather as the inevitable role that the United States had assumed in the pursuit of world order and stability—a sort of updated version of Luce's American Century.

Given the widespread concern with U.S. policy as a new assertion of imperialism, I thought it would be useful to undertake a reexamination of the various theories of imperialism and the literature on contemporary U.S. foreign policy. My working assumption was that an updating of the Marxist-Leninist theory of imperialism, giving due weight to contemporary international as well as domestic *political* factors, would provide a more coherent understanding of the motives and objectives of U.S. foreign policy. I stress the "political" for, generally speaking, Marxist-Leninist analysis has been preoccupied with the economic process, neglecting intensive analysis of international political factors, whereas scholars of the international political process have tended to deal less systematically with economic factors. There appeared to be a need, in other words, to bridge the gap between two distinct approaches. Moreover, since the Marxist-Leninist theory of imperialism, on my reading, is integrally bound up with the idea of revolution, I hypothesized that a reexamination of the theory would produce some insights into the possibilities of radical change in American society.

My prospectus was, regrettably, overoptimistic, but critical analysis of the various theories of imperialism and the literature on foreign policy did clarify my thinking. I hope this essay may provide some measure of analytic clarity, which is a prerequisite for comprehending American involvement in Indochina, and for effective political action. I cannot claim to have developed a more coherent framework for explaining American foreign policy or to have provided solid indications ("predictions"?) of radical change in American society or foreign policy. The "neo-Marxist" argument is impressive up to a point, but so is the "neo-realist," the traditional historical approach to imperialism, as I will argue below. Their premises and projections are contradictory but in a curious way complementary. Neither in itself is wholly convincing. Perhaps they can be resolved in a higher synthesis but this I have not attempted. Moreover, scrutiny of the relationship between domestic and foreign policy, in theory and in practice, does not lend itself to cheery optimism and an upbeat conclusion. One may quite agree with the most cogent radical critiques of American society, but predictions of necessary change must face up to the severe structural limitations in the way of radical change. The possibilities for a qualitatively better life—and a more rational policy—are engendered by the society itself. Awareness of the potentials in our changing society has been dramatized by the youth culture but it is not only the youth who were—and are—aware of the possibilities. That a transformation of society can be brought about rapidly and painlessly is an illusion, but does one then simply settle for the existing reality? As one of Simone de Beauvoir's characters remarks: "You'd never do anything if you thought that nothing was possible, except what already exists."[1]

Student concern over American foreign policy provided additional stimulus for this essay. As student frustration over politics and policy mounted in the 1960's, and the various organizations that had come into being proved inadequate in developing effective opposition to the Administration, interest in Marxism, virtually nonexistent in the 1950's, was rekindled. Interest centered largely in the "social humanist" ideas of the "Young Marx," which provided the focus for discussion of the possibilities of transforming an advanced capitalist society into a more equitable, humane, and rational one. At the same time, the old-line Marxist organizations began to exercise an appeal both to radically-minded students and to students who simply wanted to get into some practical activity. Here were ready-made organization and theory. With all due respect (and support) for student concern, the acceptance of traditional lines of Marxist analysis—its clichés on the working class and jargonized concepts echoing the Communist world of Stalin—struck me as regressive, unattuned to realities in the United States, and wholly inadequate to attract a large number of students into viable organization. The Marxist-Leninist theory of imperialism, in particular, furnished a seemingly satisfying explanation of U.S. foreign policy and a guideline for radical change in America. My classroom attempt was to provide a critique of the theory, to expose what was no longer relevant, and to highlight its inade-

1. *The Mandarins* (Cleveland: Meridian, 1960), p. 211.

quacies. It seemed necessary to clear away some of the old debris to free the mind for a hard look at the present reality and to build on it and not on the accepted wisdom of the radical past. If the younger generation doesn't do it, I don't know who will.

B.S.M.

Belgrade
April, 1973

Imperialism and Revolution

An Essay for Radicals

I

Introduction

Radical critics of American society and foreign policy have a special obligation to develop a theoretical framework that would serve to explain foreign policy, including Vietnam, in the context of domestic and international politics. It is also incumbent on them to elucidate the nature of the domestic changes they have in mind, the possibility of such changes, and the effect of such changes on the nature and conduct of foreign policy. Why is America following an "imperialist" policy? Is it because of fundamental flaws in our society, demanding a "revolution" in the sense of drastic change, violent or nonviolent? If so, who will make the revolution, how will it take place, what will be the specific content of "revolution" or "radical change" in American society?

The conventional Marxist response is that the "contradictions" of capitalism will inevitably lead to its transformation into socialism[1], implying a sharp break with the aims and methods of inherited foreign policy. The Marxist prognosis, dealing in indeterminate historical periods, cannot be proved or disproved. One can agree or disagree on tendencies that appear to support the Marxist theses. But

1. This is, of course, oversimplified. "There is no such thing as a general theory of the transition between social systems," wrote Paul M. Sweezy in "The Transition to Socialism," *Monthly Review*, Vol. 23, No. 1 (May 1971), p. 1; see also his "Toward a Program of Studies of the Transition to Socialism," *Monthly Review*, Vol. 23, No. 9 (February 1972), pp. 1–13.

the Marxists are loath to give proper weight to contemporary evidence or shorter-run trends that seem to run counter to their argument; they tend to interpret these trends as temporary phenomena that will work themselves out in the long run according to the Marxist perspective. Can one be blind, however, to the changing nature of the American working force and to the fact that the putative radical class, the workers, is actually supporting imperialism for its own advantage? This represents the American variant of "social-imperialism"[2]; in America, construction and aircraft workers support U.S. foreign policy and "defense policy" to assure their jobs and well-being. It is somewhat unfair to lump all Marxists together, for such sophisticated Marxist scholars as the late Paul Baran are certainly not blind to the phenomenon. In his *The Political Economy of Growth* Baran wrote that under the banner of full employment, monopoly capital can secure mass support (labor, farmer, general public) for its imperialist policies, but argued that this reliance on military spending for prosperity and high employment cannot be maintained indefinitely.[3] Perhaps he is correct, but his analysis is not convincing, relying overmuch on "in the long run," "the common man is bound to," etc.

Moreover, must or can change in this most advanced industrial society take the form of an all-out assault on the established order? In a society as relatively stable as this one, in which dissent historically has usually been dissipated by cooptation and adaptation through existing po-

2. "Social-imperialism," an attempt by the governing class to persuade the working class and the electorate that imperialist policies would work to their advantage, has had its German, Italian, French, and English variants. See, e. g., Bernard Semmel's *Imperialism and Social Reform, English Social-Imperial Thought 1895–1914* (Garden City, N.Y.: Anchor, 1968) and bibliography. But see Hugh Stretton's questioning of the concept of a popular imperialism in his *The Political Sciences* (London: Routledge and Kegan Paul, 1969), p. 132.

3. Paul A. Baran, *The Political Economy of Growth* (New York: Monthly Review Press, 1957), pp. 119 ff.

litical institutions, is it at all realistic to view revolution through the prism of the French, or Russian, or Chinese revolutions, which are the radical's historical referents? Or is revolution in modern industrial society, rooted in a strong economic base, more a matter of structural reform that would bring about distributive justice, for example, gradually incorporating values that are in consonance with "post-capitalist" society? In short, is an assault on all established institutions a *sine qua non* for significant change— and is it feasible? Alternately, can institutions and values be changed through a process of structural reform—or has American society become too rigid and oppressive to admit of radical change within the system?

Clearly some intellectual constructs rooted in the realities of present circumstances are required for perspective on our times. Spontaneity and activism are insufficient, as the record of the American New Left movement of the 1960's shows. Although the movement developed a position with regard to life-style, modes of activity, etc., yet a sympathetic commentator[4] finds that it did not succeed in developing "a new theoretical synthesis, which would include an analysis of the structures of American society, a vision of future society, and the ways and means for bringing about the transformation. . . ."[5] Thus the movement did succeed in breaking through the inertia of American politics but it did not sustain its drive in changing circumstances. It wound up as a movement without direction, goals, organization, or leadership.

Similarly in Europe, the celebration of spontaneity by such activists as Cohn-Bendit[6] proved to be premature. When the chips were down, when French society seemed

4. Massimo Teodori, *The New Left: A Documentary History* (Indianapolis and New York: Bobbs-Merrill, 1969), p. 36.

5. Ibid., pp. 80 ff.

6. Daniel Cohn-Bendit and Gabriel Cohn-Bendit, *Obsolete Communism, The Left Wing Alternative*, tr. Arnold Pomerans (London: André Deutsch, 1968).

to have been brought to a halt, the movement collapsed. Spontaneity has its limitations when it comes to sustaining a movement for radical change. Evidence that the lesson has not been lost on the students is reflected in the on-going studies of the ideas of the student movement during the 1960's and the reappraisal of the applicability of Marxist theory to American conditions by such groups as "Radical America" and others. Any such theoretical effort must ruthlessly cut away at concepts that simply do not reflect American conditions and do not face squarely the international realities of the times. Marxists routinely affirm the dynamic quality of their theory but all too often are reluctant to part with the tried and not so true. The mantle of orthodoxy is not easily discarded, and the habit of clinging to it has been a drag on innovative ideas that reflect American conditions.

One of the small ironies in the literature of the cold war is the current attribution of the term "imperialism," once reserved to describe Soviet policy, to U.S. foreign policy. Books and articles on Soviet/Communist imperialism, on blueprints for world conquest, and on totalitarianism as the modern virulent manifestation of imperialism have decreased in number while those characterizing U.S. policy as imperialist by authors who are by no means pro-Communist have multiplied. Even the 1968 Soviet invasion of Czechoslovakia did not reverse the trend. Although most observers were surprised by the Soviet action, presumably because they believed the Soviet leaders had outgrown such grotesqueries, the invasion was not out of character with previous Soviet behavior. Yet the enormity of the Soviet invasion somehow paled in the light of the American escalation of the war on Vietnam.

American writing on Soviet and U.S. foreign policy has, in fact, undergone significant changes in recent years. Although they still differ sharply with regard to the motivation, conduct, and objectives of the Soviet leadership, the tendentious output of the "hard-liners" has come under increasing criticism even by moderates.[7] Conceptual frameworks of Soviet totalitarianism and Communist monolithism have been displaced by national interest, power-politics and comparative approaches. The "special" character of the Soviet system has been de-emphasized as a factor in shaping its foreign policy. The development of a "system" of states under Soviet tutelage in East-Central Europe has posed new problems of analysis and classification.[8] The focus on satellization of the East-Central European countries in the 1940's and 50's has shifted to investigation of system characteristics, nationalist tendencies, and trends toward autonomy and polycentrism.

On the surface, nevertheless, an "imperialist" relationship does exist between the U.S.S.R. and the other Communist states. The U.S.S.R. has used, and does use, its economic and military power to determine or influence the political and economic contours of the East-Central European states—doubtless a form of imperialism. But as Sternberg pointed out many years ago,[9] the Soviet experience differs from capitalist imperialism in vital respects. Capital export has not been a motivating factor of Soviet foreign policy, and Soviet social policy in the East-Central European states has been aimed at destroying semifeudal and capitalist forces and building up large-scale industry. To comprehend the specific character of Soviet imperialism, it would be necessary to undertake an analysis of the Soviet system within the context of the world situation and the

7. See the painstaking study by William Welch, *American Images of Soviet Foreign Policy* (New Haven: Yale University Press, 1970).

8. See Jan F. Triska and David D. Finley, *Soviet Foreign Policy* (New York: Macmillan, 1968), Chapter V.

9. Fritz Sternberg, *Capitalism and Socialism on Trial*, tr. Edward Fitzgerald (New York: John Day, 1950), pp. 521 ff.

particular effects of Soviet policy in the other Communist states. On the face of it, for example, Soviet policy does not appear to have been systematically exploitative in all cases. A theory of noncapitalist imperialism would surely help in explaining the workings and tendencies of the Communist system.[10]

By contrast, there has been an outpouring of books and articles noting—and mostly regretting—the "imperialist"[11] tendencies in U.S. foreign policy. The term has not received vigorous definition; it is readily used as a synonym for interventionism and globalism. "Imperialism" seems to fit such U.S. actions as protection of American business interests in underdeveloped countries, limited intervention in the Dominican Republic, and prolonged war in Indochina to insure political arrangements in that region favorable to presumed American interests. Criticism of American policy generally follows pragmatic lines, deploring the overextension of U.S. positions and reliance on military assistance programs and military solutions. Much of it, I suspect, is *ex post* criticism of policy that has not worked out well, primarily in Indochina.[12] In any case, there is little attempt to deal with the concept of imperialism systematically in order to develop an explanatory framework for American policy. For all their intelligent observations, what the liberal critics suggest is merely that the United States do less—not a bad suggestion as far as it goes; that the United States pursue what Gati has called a "limita-

10. Cf. George Lichtheim, *Imperialism* (New York: Praeger, 1971), p. 136.
11. This is not to slight American writers of Marxian persuasion, who have been at it for some time. Appropriate references will be made below. Of course, Soviet writers have not neglected the subject. See, for example, the publication of the International Relations Publishing House, *Diplomatiya Sovremennogo Imperializma: Lyudi, Problemy, Metody*, ed. Yu. V. Borisov, A. A. Gromyko, and V. L. Israelian (Moscow, 1969).
12. On the responsibility of the liberals for Vietnam, and their failure as an intellectual class, see William Pfaff, "A Case against Interventionism" in Irving Howe, ed., *A Dissenter's Guide to Foreign Policy* (Garden City, N.Y.: Anchor, 1968). "Vietnam is the fulfillment of a kind of vulgar liberalism. . . ." (p. 100).

tionist" policy.[13] Implicit in their criticism is the assumption that the United States has considerable freedom of choice in its policy-making; implicit certainly is the belief that there is nothing inherent in the fabric of American society or in the structure of international relations that requires it to pursue an imperialist policy.[14]

Even if the non-Marxist critical literature falls short of an adequate explanation of the mainsprings of U.S. foreign policy, why turn to the concept of imperialism, which, as one scholar noted, "is no word for scholars. It has been analyzed too often, given too many shades of meaning"?[15] Yet its use persists because it capsulizes the idea of domination and control. The idea is clear; the mechanism is not. The word "imperialism" was introduced into the English language only in the 1840's, to describe the ways by which the Empire of Louis Napoleon maintained its hold on the French.[16] This would seem to preclude its application to the period before the nineteenth century and, indeed, to instances of foreign domination. But, as Koebner and Schmidt have pointed out, the word has changed its meaning "no less than twelve times" since then and its first meaning has been lost to the present generation. The meaning of the word has changed with changing circumstances, so that both outright possession of a colony and satellite relationships, Communist-style, are characterized

13. Charles Gati, "Another Grand Debate? The Limitationist Critique of American Foreign Policy," *World Politics*, Vol. XXI, No. 1 (October 1968), pp. 133–151.

14. See, for example, Ronald Steel's exhortation: "There is no more urgent task for United States diplomacy than to find a path away from the benevolent imperialism of Pax Americana and toward a reconciliation with a world shattered into a plurality of nation states." *Pax Americana* (New York: Viking, 1967), p. 336. Cf. Gabriel Kolko's review of Steel's *A Chronicle of the American Empire* (New York: Random House, 1971) in *New York Times Book Review*, September 12, 1971, p. 6.

15. A. P. Thornton, *The Imperial Idea and Its Enemies* (Garden City, N.Y.: Anchor, 1968), p. x, noting W. K. Hancock's *Wealth of Colonies*, p. 17.

16. Richard Koebner and Helmut Dan Schmidt, *Imperialism, The Story and Significance of a Political Word, 1840–1960* (Cambridge: Cambridge University Press, 1964), pp. xiii and 1.

as imperialism. And, by the same token, the word could be retrojected into the past to characterize the Carthaginian and Roman conquests.

Etymology aside, "imperialism" denotes a theory of international relations which shares some common modalities throughout history but some of whose mechanisms (not necessarily all) differ in different historical periods. Thus, although imperialist theories, particularly in the twentieth century, have been associated with Marxists and those influenced by Marxists, it is nonetheless true that other, non-Marxist theories vie with them in attempting to explain international phenomena. They meet on the common ground of theories of Great Power[17] behavior, on how the Great Powers exercise their power and influence, and on how the Great Powers attempt to promote a world order beneficial to themselves. The theoretical explanations differ widely, but they converge in focusing on the phenomena of Great Power conquest, control, domination, and exploitation of weaker peoples.

Conceptually speaking, however, Marxist theory has cast a wider net than traditional theories of international relations by attempting to integrate domestic factors with foreign behavior. Long before American political science discovered the "linkages" between domestic and foreign policy, Marxist theories of imperialism dealt with the integral connections between the two. Marxist theory even posits foreign policy as a function of domestic policy, the characteristics of the socio-economic system "determining" the nature of the foreign policy. This is not to say that non-Marxist writers have been oblivious to the influence of domestic politics and policy on foreign policy—the pressure of purely domestic political factors on American foreign policy is a datum recorded in the textbooks—but rather that rarely have American writers attempted to in-

17. Great Powers, or relatively advantaged Powers: Belgium, e.g., in the carving up of Africa.

tegrate domestic and foreign factors into a coherent theory of policy-making and its consequences on both the international and American scenes.[18] One could do worse than note Lenin's dictum in 1916 that:

> It is fundamentally wrong, un-Marxist and unscientific, to single out "foreign policy" from policy in general, let alone counterpose foreign policy to home policy. Both in foreign and home policy imperialism strives towards violations of democracy, towards reaction. In this sense, imperialism is indisputably the "negation" of *democracy in general*, of *all democracy*, and not just of *one* of its demands, national self-determination.[19]

Major decisions on foreign policy are related to the domestic structure, and the consequences of foreign policy decisions in turn affect the domestic structure. That there is reciprocal interaction seems as obvious as the inability of both Marxist and traditional models of international relations to pinpoint the cause-effect relationships. Moreover, explicit or implicit to the Marxist explanation of imperialism as a function of the domestic socio-economic system is the argument that revolutionary change in the domestic structure and in the consciousness of the exploited classes is a precondition for change in the course of foreign policy. It is this nexus between foreign policy and domestic "revolution" that still provides an inspiration for old-style Marxist organizations in the United States, but it has also kindled interest among the youth who are searching for explanations of policy. Even those in the "counter-culture" who reject, or are oblivious to, Marx are nevertheless caught up in the fundamental problem he posed of the relationship between consciousness and change.

The idea of radical change in the United States through

18. One systematic undertaking is *Linkage Politics, Essay on the Convergence of National and International Systems*, ed. James N. Rosenau (New York: Free Press, 1969).

19. "A Caricature of Marxism and Imperialist Economism," in *Lenin on the United States* (New York: International Publishers, 1970), p. 290.

the permeation of a "counter-culture" is, in effect, the old problem of consciousness in modern dress. With Marx, Lukacs, and Marcuse it seems superfluous to have Charles A. Reich on consciousness, but the merit of his work, however fatuous it seemed to many, including students, is that it presents a very American exposition of the role of consciousness in contemporary society. The categories of a Marxian theory of imperialism, then, as distinguished from the more traditional theories of imperialism, embrace not only foreign policy but its linkage to domestic policy and, in the process of analysis, purport to reveal the tendencies in capitalist society that move toward radical change.

In this book I attempt to reassess whether theories of imperialism have anything to offer, in original or updated version, in explaining American policy and its domestic and foreign consequences.

But "why the preoccupation with theory," asked one intelligent, typically American, reader. "If a man is in pain, he doesn't theorize about it, he tries to make the pain go away." (Ask any alcoholic.) The point is that one is not quite certain about what causes the pain—in this case, pain arising from foreign policy decisions. Those who feel that the fault lies with the executive branch of government would like to reorganize the Congress, or, at least, to strengthen its watchdog role in foreign policy. Others feel that the corporations are the prime source of our involvement abroad and hence opt for socialization.[20] Certainly, some theoretical perspective is necessary to provide a coherent explanation of the situation and to structure appropriate action, even though, as Hugh Stretton noted in his most suggestive analysis of various theories of imperialism, different values will require different explanatory patterns.[21]

20. See, for example, David Horowitz, ed., *Corporations and the Cold War* (New York and London: Monthly Review Press, 1969).
21. *The Political Sciences*, p. 165.

Linkage of theory and practice is integral to the radical tradition.[22] But beyond this, theory is no exercise in the void: it not only tries to explain existing reality but is also an essential tool of reformers and revolutionaries. Those who attempt to influence other people's lives bear a grave responsibility. Action in a theoretical void may very well be harmful and self-destructive. Without prejudice to the notion of spontaneous action to generate a revolutionary movement, which is all that may be possible in certain bitter social situations, action merely for the sake of action in a society as highly structured as the American can lead (and has led) to counterpressure and repression by seemingly overwhelming forces. The argument for theory as the necessary underpinning for practice may very well serve as a rationalization for doing nothing; one must be alert to this possibility. At the same time, it is foolish to cling to theories that are patently inoperative in the present scene, simply in order to have a security blanket. An outworn framework of reference is inhibiting and surely no more useful than no framework at all.

What follows in the next three chapters is a discussion essentially of the contemporary relevance of the Marxist-Leninist theory of imperialism contrasted with a contemporary version of traditional theory as applied to American foreign policy.

22. Thus, for example, Robert Wolfe's article, "American Imperialism and the Peace Movement": "One of the weaknesses of the American peace movement as presently constituted is that it lacks a clearly defined theory of imperialism." *Studies on the Left,* Vol. VI, No. 3 (May–June, 1966), reprinted in K. T. Fann and Donald C. Hodges, eds., *Readings in U.S. Imperialism* (Boston: Porter Sargent, 1971), pp. 311–325. Or Gabriel Kolko: "To some critical extent, and as difficult as that task may be, sustained structural analysis and theory must precede commitment in depth to one or another mode of tactics and action." *The Roots of American Foreign Policy* (Boston: Beacon, 1969), pp. 134–35; also pp. 48–49.

II

Marxist Theories of Imperialism

Among classic theories of imperialism—by Hobson, Schumpeter, Arendt, and by the Marxists Bukharin, Luxemburg, Kautsky, and Hilferding—Lenin's figures most prominently in whatever intellectual traffic there is on the subject. Marx himself had no general theory of imperialism, but those who followed in his tradition drew on his methodology and his general analysis of the tendencies of capitalism. Characteristic of the Marxist approach is the proposition that the inherent dynamics of capitalism shape the behavior of the state and that its foreign political and economic relations—imperialism—are a function of the capitalist system rather than, as others would have it, a function of certain "laws" deduced from the historical behavior of nation states. Lenin's *Imperialism, The Highest Stage of Capitalism* (1916), incorporating particularly Hilferding's ideas of finance capitalism and the liberal Hobson's analysis of English imperialism, became the authoritative Marxist statement on imperialism. On the contemporary scene, the late Paul Baran, Paul Sweezy, Harry Magdoff, and Ernest Mandel are leading exponents of a Marxist theory of imperialism or perhaps, more strictly, a neo-Marxist updating of Lenin's theory of imperialism.

In January 1916 Lenin was commissioned by Parus, a

legal publishing house in Petrograd, to write a book on imperialism.[1] This provided him with the opportunity, as Stretton has pointed out,[2] for a theoretical restatement and updating of Marxism to account for certain patent inadequacies in the theory, notably the failure of revolution to occur in the maturing capitalist economies and the progressive integration of the working classes into their respective systems. Was Marx's prediction of an inevitable internal conflict stemming from the contradictions between the productive apparatus and the exploited workers incorrect, necessitating the scrapping of the theory? Or were there certain intervening events, which, properly factored into Marx's line of analysis, would serve to preserve the orthodox Marxist theory and, consequently, the prospect of socialist revolution? Lenin's contemporaries provided various explanations. Karl Kautsky, for example, viewed imperialism as a policy—rather than an inevitability—that suited industrial capitalism, and even advanced the possibility of capitalism's developing into a single world monopoly, "ultra-imperialism."[3] Lenin, lambasting Kautsky, clung to the orthodox view of inevitable internal revolution resulting from the contradictions between the socialized relations of production and private appropriation and held to the view that the exploited proletariat would be the revolutionary agent.

What Lenin did was to take Marx's model of "industrial" or "competitive" capitalism and expand it into a more complex system of "monopoly" capitalism in order to account for developments in the capitalist system since

1. V. I. Lenin, *Collected Works*, Vol. 39: *Notebooks on Imperialism*, tr. Clemens Dutt (Moscow: Progress Publishers, 1968; London: Lawrence and Wishart), p. 771.

2. *The Political Sciences*, Chapter 4.

3. Tom Kemp, *Theories of Imperialism* (London: Dobson, 1967), pp. 76–77. A very useful analysis of various theories of imperialism. Cf. John H. Kautsky's article "J. A. Schumpeter and Karl Kautsky: Parallel Theories of Imperialism," *Midwest Journal of Political Science*, Vol. V, No. 2 (May 1961), pp. 101–128.

Marx had written about it in mid-nineteenth century. Lenin's exposition is sufficiently familiar so as to require no more than the barest summary here. The "modern" or "highest" stage of capitalism, as it was termed in the essay,[4] was characterized by the combination and merger of industry into trusts and cartels and, additionally, by the enlargement and combination of the banking system. The banks, in turn, penetrated the business enterprises and contributed heavily to their capital. This new phase of finance capital introduced new contradictions into the system over and above Marx's model. Production and profits were temporarily regulated. But monopoly served to restrict production and depress wages. The greater productive capacity of the international trusts was restricted in order to increase profits. Temporary relief was afforded by exporting capital, taking the form of what Kemp has called the "struggle for economic territory." That is, capitalists, supported by their respective governments, sought exclusive preserves as sources of raw materials, markets, and investment opportunities. As a consequence, the years before 1914 witnessed the division of the world by a few European powers, the exaction of enormous profits by the monopolies, and, as a by-product, years of relative peace while the world was being divided up. The conditions and standard of living of the working class improved (though it is not clear that this could be attributed solely to imperialism; scholars disagree).

The effect of relative peace and prosperity during this phase of imperialist expansion was to induce a mood of opportunism and reformism in the socialist movement, creating, according to Lenin, a group or stratum among the labor bureaucracy and petty-bourgeois fellow travelers who paid only lip service to revolutionary aims and revolutionary tactics. Superprofits gleaned from the colonies had been

4. V. I. Lenin, *Imperialism: The Highest Stage of Capitalism* (New York: International Publishers, 1939).

used to buy off the leaders of the working class. When the rivalries of the imperialist powers finally exploded into war, the proletariat, instead of capitalizing on the opportunity for revolutionary action, was beguiled against its true interests by the socialist and labor leaders into supporting its respective bourgeois governments.

Marx had posited the possibility of socialist revolution developing organically from the internal mechanisms of capitalism. The progressive refinement of the productive and organizational techniques of capitalism would supersede the individualistic organization of production, holding the proletariat at subsistence level and creating reservoirs of unemployment. This situation would engender intolerable social tension to a point at which the proletariat, having become conscious both of its exploited role and of the possibilities of a qualitatively better system which the productive capacity of capitalism afforded, would then seize power. The seizure of power by the proletariat, the overwhelmingly largest class in the system, would open up the prospect for a classless, socialist society.

It might be noted parenthetically that for an analyst, observing the process of industrialization in England and the Continent in the mid-nineteenth century, the designation of the proletariat as the "historical agent" of revolution was a logical possibility (quite apart from the "moral" necessity of a proletarian takeover). The displacement of peasants on the land, the squeezing out of small entrepreneurs and craftsmen, the enrollment of large numbers in the industrial army—and their exploitation—all pointed in this direction. The point is worth noting—and we shall return to it—because of the fixation on the revolutionary potential of the working class from Marx's day, when it did seem plausible, to the present, when advanced industrial society is wiping out the type of worker Marx had in mind.

Lenin's revolutionary theory was very much in the framework of Marx's, with imperialism as the added dimension.[5] The internal organic workings of capitalism engendered precisely the contradictions leading to revolution envisioned by Marx, except for the prolongation of the incubation period because the capitalists and financiers found in overseas investment a temporary outlet to stave off the inevitable. This had an "unfortunate" effect on a portion of the working class and on the timing of the revolution, but the socialist revolution remained historically inevitable and the working class was the chosen instrument.

In sum, Lenin argued that it was a matter of necessity— not of policy, choice, or taste—that, under conditions of monopoly, capitalism sought outlets in the colonies in order to secure profits. This economic necessity unavoidably became a political necessity as well, because of the class nature of the system. Since the capitalists constituted the ruling class of the state by virtue of their ownership of the means of production, they could use the instruments of state power to protect their investments. The competition for economic territory would lead to interstate conflict and war. How else, Lenin asked, were serious conflicts between nation-states settled? Finally, war would provide the breeding ground for revolution. The proletarians would understand that they were the real victims of war, that they had nothing to gain and everything to lose (their lives) and they would come to realize that they had been bought off by a mess of imperialist pottage.[6] Despite an era of relative peace

5. The reader is undoubtedly aware of the contrary view, i.e., that Leninism represents a sharp break with Marxism.

6. How passionately the Bolsheviks believed this! Nikolai Bukharin, a year before Lenin's *Imperialism*, wrote: "The war severs the last chain that binds the workers to the masters, their slavish submission to the imperialist state. The last limitation of the proletariat's philosophy is being overcome; its clinging to the narrowness of the national state, its patriotism. The interests of the moment, the temporary advantage accruing to it from the imperialist robberies and from its connections with the imperialist state, become of secondary importance compared with the lasting and general interests of the class as a whole, with the idea of a social revolution of the international proletariat which overthrows the dictatorship of finance capital with an armed hand, destroys its state apparatus and builds up a new power, a power of the workers against the bourgeoisie. In place of the idea

and an improvement in the condition of the proletariat, the workings of the capitalist system were directed against it. Lenin's theory, then, is an integral theory of capitalist imperialism, war, and revolution with the proletariat as the mediating agent. As an explanatory framework, it stands or falls on the interrelationship of these three phenomena, quite apart from the validity of any particular insights into the mechanism of the capitalist system.

Lenin's theory of imperialism, moreover, is a theory of revolution in advanced capitalist countries—not in the colonies or backward areas. The association of Lenin's theory with the breaking of the capitalist chain at its "weakest link" is not borne out by Lenin's essay itself, nor by the extensive notebooks[7] he compiled in preparation for the essay. The notion of the "weakest link" is at best an *ex post* rationalization for the Bolshevik revolution in semi-industrial Russia, which has received further support through the revolution in semi-industrial China and has since been translated into the conception of the eventual disintegration of the capitalist system by the progressive "drop-out" of the backward areas. Although it is an incontrovertible fact that Russia, China, the East-Central European and Asian Communist states have dropped out of the capitalist system, the explanation therefor cannot be derived from Lenin's theory of imperialism. The explanation is somewhere else. The point is not an idle one in reviewing Lenin's theory of imperialism for any light it may cast on the mechanics of present-day imperialism. For he was—and we are—concerned with the potential for change in the dominant capitalist countries, and whatever explanation Lenin

of defending or extending the boundaries of the bourgeois state that bind the productive forces of world economy hand and foot, this power advances the slogan of *abolishing* state boundaries and merging all the peoples into one Socialist family. In this way the proletariat, after painful searching, succeeds in grasping its true interests that lead it through revolution to Socialism." *Imperialism and World Economy* (New York: Howard Fertig, 1966), p. 167.

7. *Collected Works*, Vol. 39.

provides should, in the strictest sense, emanate from his theoretical formulations on imperialism. Elsewhere he said much on strategy and tactics in backward areas that may be pertinent, but that was elsewhere.

As to the validity of Lenin's theory, historians and economists have challenged him on such key points as the specific factors and timing leading to the acquisition of colonies. They assert, for example, that trade has more often than not followed the flag and not vice versa; that colonial expansion may not have been necessary to maintain the system because, among other factors, overseas investment constituted only a small fraction of the activity of European capitalists; and that he ignored the political factor.

Yet the attempt to refute Lenin's theses by pointing out that the greatest period of colonial expansion took place before the period with which Lenin was concerned is no argument at all. Lenin explicitly made reference to the previous imperialist period. What he was concerned with was the mechanics of capitalism as they became transformed into the "monopoly" stage. Then, too, Lenin was justified in drawing a distinction between the nature and operations of capitalism at the turn of the century and the earlier period of competitive or industrial capitalism. The fact that investment in the colonies constituted a small share of total investment does not negate the Leninist thesis, since it is the consequence of overseas expansion that was—and is—at issue. It may not be demonstrable that overseas economic expansion "saved" capitalism, but it did provide new fields of investment and sources of profit. Overseas expansion was interwoven with national policies and an extension of rivalries on the Continent. Continental and overseas rivalries were linked and did figure in the tension leading to World War I.

Nor does the charge that Lenin neglected the political factor—state policy—have much substance. How he would have elaborated on the political aspects is open to doubt but he certainly was aware of them. He was writing under censorship and had to confine himself to the economic underpinnings of capitalist expansion. As the quotation from Lenin's work cited above[8] clearly indicates, politics was inextricably bound up with economics. Was politics ever absent from Lenin's mind?

In all, Lenin's theory did provide a plausible explanatory framework for capitalism in its "modern" phase and for the tensions generated by its activities in contributing to national rivalries that figured in the outbreak of World War I. Lenin's interest, however, was not simply in providing an exposé of the workings of capitalism or an explanation of the outbreak of the war, but primarily in providing a theory of revolution in capitalist society. It is surprising —and significant—that in the ongoing discussion of imperialism, the prospect of revolution within capitalist society has been neglected in serious theoretical discussion. This is understandable on the part of those liberal critics of American foreign policy who freely use the word "imperialism" pejoratively to express their displeasure with the means and style of policy. But they do not offer a structural concept of imperialism; their remedies are generally temporizing ones—limiting objectives, internationalizing aid, etc. It is striking, however, that those who have reexamined radical theories of imperialism for relevance to the contemporary scene have little to say about the implications for revolution in Marxist theory. Part of the explanation, perhaps, is that those commentators, writing in a more or less democratic socialist tradition, have long since rejected the possibility of revolution Marxist-style.[9]

The explanation for the neglect of the revolutionary factor within an organic theory of imperialism by "Old Left" Marxists and the "New Left" is more puzzling. For with-

8. P. 19, note 9.

9. See, e.g., Henry Pachter, "The Problem of Imperialism," *Dissent*, September–October 1970, pp. 461–488.

out the implications for revolution, discussion of Marxist theories of imperialism is little more than an intellectual exercise. This may be an exaggeration: analysis of imperialism that throws any light on the mechanism of capitalism is useful. But what then? Clearly the thrust behind a Marxist theory of capitalism is the potential for radical change, and it is clear that the thrust behind Lenin's theory was the revolutionary potential inherent in capitalist imperialism. Just as Hobson developed a theory of imperialism to argue for a change in English policy, so Lenin offered a theoretical framework for revolutionary change. His was no mere intellectual exercise.

Crucial to Lenin's theory of imperialism is the role of the working class. His concern with the reformist tendencies in the socialist movement was already evident at the turn of the century. This much he had in common with Eduard Bernstein[10]: recognition of the pacification of the English and West European working class as a result of such developments as the rising standard of living and progressive integration into capitalist society through enfranchisement, protection of working-class organization, and various social welfare measures. But unlike Bernstein, who was prepared to settle for "evolutionary socialism" at the expense of discarding, de facto, the entire Marxist baggage, Lenin was committed to achieving a socialist revolution. His focus was understandably upon Russia but conditions in Russia were not propitious for the development of a large, class-conscious proletariat that would act out its historical responsibilities. Moreover, Lenin's writings reflect his suspicion that a maturing working class would, in fact, become nonrevolutionary. Lenin consequently argued for the creation in Russia of an elite corps of professional revolutionaries as a necessary organizational form to function at all effectively under conditions of the Tsarist autocracy.

10. *Evolutionary Socialism,* tr. Edith C. Harvey (New York: Schocken, 1961).

In so doing, he attempted to stay within the Marxist framework, first by making clear (in *What Is To Be Done*, for example) that he was not rejecting the mass-type Marxist party of the West; the organizational form that had developed in western Europe was simply inapplicable to Russia. Secondly, he could plead his orthodoxy by linking his concept of an organizational elite to Marx's own Communist League, which had as one of its main functions the education of the workers in socialism, and, more specifically, to Marx's appeal for the formation of secret workers' organizations in addition to other forms of working-class association after the failure of the revolutionary actions of 1848–49[11].

The significance of Lenin's organizational innovation for revolutionary theory is not that he paved the way for the dictatorship of the Communist party and of Stalin (though perhaps he did) but that he profoundly challenged —appeals to Marxist orthodoxy to the contrary notwithstanding—one of the basic tenets of Marxist revolutionary theory, that is, the development of conscious revolutionary purpose among the masses. The significance of Lenin's innovation is large not only for its effect on the organizational concept of the Communist International but more significantly on the very concept of revolutionary consciousness in Marx and in our own time. If the nineteenth-century working class was unable to achieve a consciousness of its own role in capitalist society, both of its oppression by the system and of its liberation from that system, in order to effect a socialist transformation, then Marx's psychology would appear to have been faulty. That the working class would break through the "false" reality of its condition was an implication of Marx's dialectical reasoning which has not been historically justified. That

11. Karl Marx and Frederick Engels, "Address of the Central Committee to the Communist League," in *Marx-Engels, Selected Works*, Vol. 1 (Moscow: Foreign Languages Publishing House, 1962), pp. 106–117.

the working class would come to know its own interests is no more than an article of faith which simply does not take into account the conservatizing forces of material welfare and the un-Promethean nature of man.

The proletarian, forced to work long hours, six or six and a half days a week, living with his family at subsistence level, might take to revolutionary action for the same reasons that a Bolivian peasant might join a guerrilla movement. It would represent an act of desperation in a situation of little choice. But in Marxian theory it was not desperation alone that propelled the worker to revolutionary action; it was also—and necessarily—a cognitive grasp of his existential condition and of the idea of a new socialist reality. How much more difficult, then, for the worker who is experiencing some of the benefits of society to break with what he already has in order to bring into reality the abstraction of a "good society." Marx was asking too much. The "necessity" for a qualitatively better society, the underlying thrust of Marx's critique of capitalism, was not within the comprehension of the proletariat—one might say it was beyond their belief (or, for that matter, of those Marxist socialists who opted for reformism).

Marx's profound moral vision was beyond the historical capability of the proletariat. Formally, various strands of evolutionary and orthodox Marxism did not abandon the idea of the proletariat as the revolutionary agent, contending that it was a matter of education and time, but the overwhelming patriotic response of the socialists and working class in World War I spelled the demise of what might be called Western revolutionary socialism. How then to account for the durability of Lenin's theory of imperialism?

The transmutation of Lenin's theory of imperialism and revolution into dogma by the Communist movement and the faith placed in the working class as the instrument of change by Communists and socialists generally have both contributed to the mystification of the problem of radical transformation of industrial society. This is obvious. But how does one assess the validity of the analysis of those highly qualified independent Marxists who still espouse Lenin's theory of imperialism—with some variations? Take Paul M. Sweezy, for example. In his *The Theory of Capitalist Development*[12], first published in 1942, he describes the features of imperialism essentially as Lenin did in his five-point definition[13]: (a) several advanced countries compete for the world market for industrial products; (b) monopoly capital, subsuming Lenin's finance capital, is the dominant form of capital; (c) capital export is an outstanding feature of world economic relations; (d) rivalry in the world market leads alternatively to cutthroat competition and to international monopoly combines; and, finally, to (e) the territorial division of what he calls the "unoccupied" part of the world. Lenin's conception of capitalism and its imperialist manifestations is thus essentially valid to Sweezy, as it is to Ernest Mandel,[14] who, in his elaborate analysis of capitalism, nevertheless, like Sweezy, fails to present an operative theory of revolution. There does not appear in these analyses a convincing statement of the "contradictions" in the system that would lead to radical change.

Or take Harry Magdoff, who has written a strongly documented analysis of the economic underpinning of Ameri-

12. New York: Monthly Review Press, 1968, p. 307.
13. *Imperialism*, p. 89.
14. *Marxist Economic Theory*, tr. Brian Pearce (New York and London: Monthly Review Press, 1968), 2 vols. Again Mandel's opinion that socialism is the only "clear way out" of Europe's dilemma, caught as it is between subjection to America and the "Americanization" that J. J. Servan-Schreiber describes (see below, p. 33, note 6.), has little more than hortatory value as a convincing explanation of working class militancy. *Europe versus America? Contradictions of Imperialism*, tr. Martin Rossdale (London: NLB, 1970), Chapter 11.

can foreign policy.[15] Presenting a wealth of data on U.S. foreign economic relations, Magdoff argues that the system requires that the political and economic principles of capitalism should prevail and that it should have an open door, if not a privileged position, for foreign investment and trade. Hence, "imperialism is not a matter of choice for a capitalist society: it is the way of life of such a society."[16] To Magdoff, then, "there is a close parallel between, on the one hand, the aggressive United States foreign policy aimed at controlling (directly and indirectly) as much of the globe as possible, and, on the other hand, an energetic internationalist expansionist policy of U.S. business."[17]

Magdoff's argument, as far as it goes, makes a great deal of sense to me, but it does not go far enough in its implications. Assuming, at least for the sake of argument, that Magdoff and others offer valid analyses of the foreign manifestations of capitalism and the linkage between economic and foreign policy, two leading questions pose themselves. First, is not the system in the interest of the vast majority of the American people? And second, where are the internal mechanisms in the system that will bring about the desired change? On this second point, Marxist analysis is weak; I shall touch upon it in Chapters III and V.

The first question is too little asked by Marxists or even by radical and liberal critics of the system. The omission is not of slight consequence: if the system serves the interest not only of the business community but also of various strata of American society, including the working class, whence, then, comes the dynamic for change? Surely it is in the interest of the American people to enjoy—and to continue to enjoy—wealth and the increasing standard of living provided under capitalism. This subsumes not only

15. *The Age of Imperialism* (New York: Monthly Review Press, 1969). See Robert W. Tucker's criticism of Magdoff in *The Radical Left and American Foreign Policy* (Baltimore: Johns Hopkins Press, 1971).

16. Ibid., p. 26.

17. Ibid., p. 12.

material wealth but the cultural and recreational opportunity, as well (leaving aside for the moment the factor of quality) that capitalism provides. If it is in the nature of capitalism to engage in all manner of overseas activities, ranging from the extraction of raw materials in underdeveloped areas to the purchase of European automobile and computer plants, so be it. If the safeguarding of overseas economic activity requires the occasional use of American muscle, that may be unfortunate—the argument would run—but it doesn't happen too often and occurs out of sight, so to speak, of the American people. Historical circumstances (and American genius?) have made the United States the richest nation in the world; why not enjoy it? Certainly there are inequities in American society and in the world but man is not perfect and the system is flexible enough gradually to improve the lot of the less fortunate. Surely this reflects the philosophy of our liberal utilitarians and, perhaps, of sections of our conservative thought as well. The Marxists claim, by contrast, that capitalism has no choice other than to be what it is.

In fact, there is a remarkable, if unintended, convergence between the Marxist critique and the status quoers. The conservative could very well accept the Marxist analysis of capitalism and fight to preserve it. The Marxist, on the other hand, may see the workings of capitalism most clearly and fight to change it. But he can fight it only if he can correctly identify the tendencies and forces in society that point to change. The contention that the system does not serve the people's real interests, that it is designed to serve "false needs," has an arrogant bit of sophistry to it. Perhaps the Marxists' conception of "needs" places society on a higher qualitative level, but try to convince the working class and the salariat. Mere moral protest against the system is insufficient if the majority of Americans is by and large content with its lot and, in addition, unable to envision a new society in which it would be better off.

Contemporary Marxists have updated Lenin's theory of imperialism, but they have not provided an organic theory of revolution in advanced capitalist countries. However valuable their illumination of the economic tendencies within the capitalist world and of the social implications of a society dominated by the quest for private gain, their insights into relations between states, etc., they have provided more of a context than a guide to action. Their analysis of the underlying tendencies of world capitalism may indeed point to change over an unspecified historical period, but whether it will be change in the social humanist direction implied by Marxist analysis is moot. Nevertheless, compared to other theories of imperialism, the neo-Marxist (the best we have) remains a suggestive line of analysis for an understanding of United States policy, though it falls short of being a convincing explanatory theory on two counts in particular: (1) the commanding role of politics in the present period beyond Lenin's idea of it, and (2) the theory of revolution or the radical transformation of advanced industrial society.

III

Critique of Marxist Theories of Imperialism

Lenin's theory of imperialism, considered as an integral theory of imperialism and revolution, simply does not stand up under contemporary circumstances. Nor have the neo-Marxist variants, as I have suggested above, presented a sufficiently strong case, particularly with regard to the countervailing forces in the national and international system that would bring about radical change. The structure of world capitalism and of world politics that underlay Lenin's analysis has changed, and with it the operational mechanisms that Lenin derived from his theory. How have they changed?

First of all, imperialism in the form of the direct domination and control of outlying areas has virtually disappeared. The colonies have become sovereign states, which, in itself, would call for a revision, if not scotching, of Leninist theory. Soviet theorists, but not only Soviet theorists, have accommodated by advancing the concept of "neo-colonialism," arguing that the form of imperialism has changed but not the substance. Although the colonies have achieved political independence, they remain economically dependent on the great capitalist states. Economic dependence implies an infringement on the sovereignty of the newly independent states, since they are not free to plan their own lives and to reallocate their resources in pursuit of their particular goals. Hence they remain in fact, if not in theory, politically subservient to capitalism.

There is little question that the freedom of newly independent states has been circumscribed by their historical experience as colonies and that their attempts at development have been frustrating. Although foreign capital did serve to develop certain industries in the colonies, broadly speaking the basic pattern has been the exploitation of indigenous resources that were complementary to the economies of the industrial states or that yielded substantial profit to the foreign entrepreneur—at the expense of the creation of a more variegated economy responsive to the colonies' needs. One outcome of this pattern has been the entrenchment of essentially one-crop economies on which these former colonies are still dependent. Concomitantly, imperial policy stunted progressive social and political development, the evolution of technical and managerial skills, etc., a catalogue the reader can easily expand.

But the situation in the newly independent countries and other poor countries that have been formally independent for years, such as those in Central America, is due not simply to the fact that they are tied to capitalism but also to the inadequacy of their own resources to set in motion a process of capital accumulation analogous to the experience of the industrial states in both the West and the Communist nations. What they require is more disinterested help from the Communist and capitalist states (far more from the richer capitalist states), but neither the political nor the business leadership of either finds it particularly in its interest to divert its respective resources to aid the underdeveloped countries in any substantial way. Marxist analysts who correctly perceive the interrelationships between capitalist imperialism and the underdeveloped countries nevertheless do not provide a convincing explanation of how the situation can be changed (or of how revolution in the advanced countries will occur through the progressive defection of underdeveloped countries to the socialist camp). Theirs is a moral plea with which one may agree but it is not "scientific" analysis, as they would have it. Thus,

> A socialist transformation of the advanced West would not only open to its own peoples the road to unprecedented economic, social and cultural progress, it would at the same time enable the peoples of the underdeveloped countries to overcome rapidly their present condition of poverty and stagnation. It would not only put an end to the exploitation of the backward countries; a rational organization and full utilization of the West's enormous productive resources would readily permit the advanced nations to repay at least a part of their historical debt to the backward peoples and to render them generous and unselfish help in their effort to increase speedily their desperately inadequate "means of employment."[1]

In fact, as the period of the cold war came to an end and the Great Powers were maneuvering into new associations and alignments in the early 1970's, the "Third World," with the exception of those countries that represented some politico-military advantage to the Great Powers, figured marginally. As one (anonymous) American official put it, economic aid for the underdeveloped countries has been placed on the "back burner"—a far cry from the cold war slogan of winning the minds and hearts of the "Third World" with economic aid.

The disparities of levels of well-being between the advanced countries (including the East-Central European Communist states) and the Third World constitute a moral problem and, perhaps, may come to represent a serious political problem between the "northern and southern tiers," but the problem is a different one from that which engaged

---

1. Baran, *The Political Economy of Growth*, p. 250.

Lenin in his theory of imperialism. Neocolonialism as a condition unquestionably exists[2], but neocolonialism as an explanation of capitalist imperialism in contemporary circumstances does not have much theoretical content. Thus, one expositor of the concept, Jack Woddis, defines neocolonialism as a "strategy" of imperialism to which the imperialists have turned as a result of the end of direct colonial rule.[3] Indirect methods of domination are not a new aspect of imperialism, he writes, but they are now refined to maintain whatever control the imperialists have in the face of the tendency of the newly independent states to turn toward socialism, now a distinct possibility as a result of the emergence of a powerful socialist camp since World War II. Essentially, however, the author conceives of neocolonialism as a collection of means, perhaps more refined than in the past, but certainly not a new theoretical concept.

The protagonists of the concept of neocolonialism recognize, at least implicitly, that the classic Leninist analysis of imperialism is out of date. Kwame Nkrumah, for example, argued that in contemporary circumstances, the revolution will take on an international character. Whereas Marx projected conflict on a national scale between the haves and have-nots, the conflict now has been transferred to the international level. In Nkrumah's words: "The danger is now not civil war within individual States provoked by intolerable conditions within those States, but international war provoked ultimately by the misery of the major-

2. "This thing neo-colonialism is not, as some people would like to tell us, a catch-phrase, an honest investor from Europe or America or whatever, dressed up by the Communists in sheets as an evil spirit's face. It is with us now in the form of 'disinterested' help given by the great powers; in the domination of our national resources by international companies; and in the perpetuation of our economic inferiority as the eternal producers of raw materials at low prices and customers for the finished product at high prices." Nadine Gordimer, *A Guest of Honor* (New York: Viking, 1970), pp. 361–362.

3. *An Introduction to Neo-Colonialism* (New York: International Publishers, 1967), pp. 50–52.

ity of mankind who daily grow poorer and poorer."[4] The danger of international war can be avoided, Nkrumah implied (he was writing in an African context), by the unity of the underdeveloped areas, which would force the capitalist powers to adjust to the new balance of world forces as they have done in the past. This is a play on Marx's slogan in the *Communist Manifesto*: Neocolonial peoples have nothing to lose but their chains. They have a world to win. Neocolonial people of all countries, unite!

This is neither to poke fun at Nkrumah, to minimize the plight of neocolonial peoples, nor to underestimate the power of slogans and Marx's slogan in particular, but again to emphasize that exhortation is not theory. The problem of achieving unity in one country, let alone in Africa, let alone in all the underdeveloped countries, and the gross disparities in power between the advanced capitalist world and the underdeveloped areas reduce the prospect of the internationalization of the revolution to mere verbiage. Nkrumah was well aware of this. He has written a political tract in the Marxist tradition and a call to action against the capitalist grip on Africa. That may have its uses. As theory, however, it does not go far, but it does implicitly illuminate the obsolescence of part of Lenin's theory.

To return to the point made at the outset: the neocolonialists argue that the form of imperialism has changed but not the substance. That is to say, direct imperialist control of the colony no longer exists but control is maintained indirectly by virtue of the imperialist state's domination of the economic life of the colony. But looking at it strictly from the point of view of Lenin's theory, *substance* has also changed, simply because colonies are no longer there to be acquired and fought over. Imperialist states may compete with each other in the former colonial areas

4. *Neo-Colonialism, The Last Stage of Imperialism* (New York: International Publishers, 1969), p. 256.

for profits and influence but it is not quite the same game. The power of decision of the capitalist states over these areas has been curtailed, and the way in which the compe- tition is carried on has changed.

Secondly, the capitalist unisystem has been destroyed. A socialist world system has emerged that automatically changes the terms of the Leninist analysis. Conflicts be- tween states in Lenin's theory took place within the capi- talist system—the only one then extant—and the major rivalry and potential for revolution were here. Rivalry and conflict tended to lead to war, which set the preconditions for socialist revolution. With the emergence of the world socialist sector, an ideological dimension has been added in which socialist versus capitalist rivalry has transcended intra-capitalist rivalry. Stalin's two-camp doctrine and American free world ideology illustrate the point. Capital- ist policy, particularly American, has been conducted in large part in response to the challenge of Communism.[5] The world conflict which Lenin saw in his *Imperialism* as economically based rivalries between capitalists has to a large extent been transformed into a political-ideological struggle between the United States and the Communist countries.

If Lenin's analysis of imperialism was valid for his time, it was not valid for the world situation that emerged after World War II. The ideological world split gave pride of place to the capitalist-Communist conflict and to political- military considerations over economic. It may be argued that Lenin certainly took the post-1917 situation into ac- count and spoke of frightful collision between Soviet Rus- sia and the capitalists, etc. But what he had in mind was the possibility of attack by the capitalists on the weak So- viet state. More to the point of theory, Lenin's pronounce-

5. I have tried to work this out in my *International Communism and American Policy* (New York: Atherton, 1966).

ments along these lines in no way constituted a theory of imperialism. Lenin's imperialism remains the theory he outlined in 1916, which still figures prominently in Soviet Marxist and non-Marxist writing alike.

Thirdly, not only has the capitalist unisystem been destroyed but the power structure among capitalist states, compared to 1916, has altered beyond recognition. After World War II, the United States emerged as a power virtually unchallengeable by the other capitalist states. The technological disparity that accompanied the military imbalance provoked such commentators as Servan-Schreiber to write of the "conquest" of Europe by the United States.[6] The disparity between the military power of the United States and the other capitalist countries simply eliminates the possibility of intercapitalist rivalry in the Leninist sense. Conflicts between capitalist countries and the United States over trade and monetary policies continue to exist but a resort to war over these and related policies does appear to be improbable.

Even in the Soviet Union, Lenin's prediction of intercapitalist conflict arising from imperialist policies was given prominent play at the highest level of government only once since World War II, to underscore a shift in strategy. In 1952, Stalin wrote that intercapitalist conflict was more possible than capitalist-Communist conflict.[7] Stalin was reaffirming Lenin's thesis not because he anticipated a repetition of pre-World-War-II intercapitalist rivalries, but because he wished to improve Soviet-American relations. The shift from the two-camp strategy to peaceful coexistence, Stalin-style, was ideologically justified by trotting out Lenin's theory. Shortly afterward both Lenin's pre-World-War-I theory of imperialism, war, and revolu-

6. J. J. Servan-Schreiber, *The American Challenge*, tr. Ronald Steel (New York: Avon, 1969), pp. 239–240.

7. *Economic Problems of Socialism in the USSR* (New York: International Publishers, 1952).

tion and the subsequent Communist doctrine of inevitable war between the capitalist and Communist systems were retired to the dustbin of history by Khrushchev.[8]

The point of this is that even in Soviet theory the consequential aspects of Lenin's theory of imperialism have been scrapped except for whatever window dressing and propaganda purposes they might serve. This is another way of saying that, in reality, the Communists concede that the structure of world capitalism has changed to the point at which the cherished theory of imperialism is inoperative. Hence the formulations beginning in the 1950's on "neo-colonialism." Sweden and Switzerland no doubt benefit from participation in the intercapitalist system, but there is no concern about them as "imperialists." The *power* of the United States is the vital factor, power that is economic, scientific, technological, and military, and the exercise of this power in the world theatre is translated into "imperialism."

The radical alteration of the structure of world power has taken place concomitantly with a qualitative change in American capitalism. The concentration of capital and the intertwining of control and ownership have developed to a point not even imagined by Lenin and in a form he did not suspect. American society is dominated by corporate interests which make the important decisions with regard to production, allocation of resources, and distribution of income. To borrow from G. Willi.m Domhoff's *Who Rules America?*, we have a governing class drawn from the upper classes, who dominate government, business, and

8. "Secret Speech of Khrushchev Concerning the 'Cult of the Individual', Delivered at the Twentieth Congress of the Communist Party of the Soviet Union, February 25, 1956," in *The Anti-Stalin Campaign and International Communism* (New York: Columbia University Press, 1956), pp. 1–89. See my discussion of Stalin's and Khrushchev's treatment of the Leninist doctrine in "Continuity of Communist Strategic Doctrine since the Twentieth Party Congress," *Annals of the American Academy of Political and Social Science*, Philadelphia, Vol. 317 (May, 1958), pp. 130–137.

politics.[9] The governing class has become so powerful as to cast doubt on the viability of the democratic process, conceived as a two-party electoral scheme operating with checks and balances achieved by various interest groups. The structure of American society has been reordered; one could argue that what exists is essentially a governing class and a pervading middle class, including most of the workers, and an "underclass" due as much to historical circumstances as to the nature of the economic system, made up of blacks and poor whites.[10] Not only has the American class structure undergone changes that throw doubt on the revolutionary agency, as seen by Marxist-Leninists, but the concentration of power in the hands of a small group in the context of a new world environment has added a political dimension that has not figured prominently in Marxist-Leninist theories of imperialism. Lenin may still be correct in pointing to the "economic essence" of imperialism, but independent political factors seem to have intruded themselves into the decision-making process.

Let us probe this point by asking to what extent economic factors have "determined," substantially influenced, major U.S. foreign policy. Let us take the case of Vietnam, the major foreign affairs preoccupation of the country during the 1960's. The historical record as we have it, including *The Pentagon Papers*, does not reflect direct concern

9. Englewood Cliffs, N.J.: Prentice-Hall, 1967. In Domhoff's definition, "A governing class is a social upper class which receives a disproportionate amount of a country's income, owns a disproportionate amount of a country's wealth, and contributes a disproportionate number of its members to the controlling institutions and key decision-making groups in that country" (p. 142). See also his subsequent work, *The Higher Circles: The Governing Class in America* (New York: Random House, 1970). It seems to me that American social scientists would have profited in their investigation of the American power structure by pursuing the lines of analysis developed by C. Wright Mills and Domhoff rather than their preoccupations with "pluralism" and "consensus."

10. I am quite aware that, politically speaking, matters are more complex; that divisions and alliances cut across these class lines, e.g., in the "underclass" between blacks and whites.

with economic advantage. This, in itself, is not necessarily conclusive. The governing class may well have concealed its economic interests behind a cloud of ideological verbiage. Thus, even if the United States did not have a pre-existing economic stake in Indochina which it felt obliged to protect, it has been argued nevertheless that the U.S. action was preemptive.[11] This is to say, by insuring the non-Communist character of South Vietnam and of Southeast Asia, the United States maintained economic access to these areas.[12] Call it the current version of the Open Door Policy[13] or, in the Nixonian context, "protective custody." Such an argument, however, comes close to being reductionist, leaving unexplained many intervening factors, for any action to keep an area out of Communist hands can then be said to be motivated by economic interest. But whether it was or not can be decided only on the basis of empirical evidence. Even if economic advantage accrues from a particular action, considerations other than economic may in fact have determined the decision-making— and this seems to have been the case in Vietnam.

The record shows that successive American administrations, from Eisenhower to Nixon, believed it important for strategic and ideological reasons to keep South Vietnam and Southeast Asia out of Communist hands. As a simple matter of global strategy, it was not in the interests of the United States to allow one area or another to fall into Communist hands, especially into the sphere of a large Communist power, such as the People's Republic of China. The argument that American power was not materially affected by the ultimate disposition of South Vietnam—that the United States had at its disposal sufficient capability to de-

11. See, e.g., Carl Oglesby and Roger Shaull, *Containment and Change* (New York: Macmillan, 1967).

12. Magdoff makes a strong case for the interrelationship and mutually supporting political, military, and economic aspects, discounting the importance of "which comes first." *The Age of Imperialism*, pp. 165–167.

13. To borrow from Professor William Appleman Williams.

ter any aggressor—misses the point. The preservation or maximization of power is sufficient cause to any governing class that continues to play the old game of international politics. It may be true that by maintaining its position the United States secures its economic possibilities, but the point is secondary in terms of the motivations of the American leaders insofar as they are ascertainable from action and rhetoric. The ability to affect decisions in any part of the world increases the sense of security. Conversely, inability to affect decisions decreases the sense of security, as is obvious in the Middle East with the decline of Western influence, and as is the case (or will be the case) as American power is eroded in Southeast Asia.

To put it another way, it is not capitalism *per se* that drives the United States into aggressive actions, it is rather that aggressive action stems from American power, which does happen to have a capitalist base. A noncapitalist Soviet Union invaded Czechoslovakia for political and military reasons. It may have been securing its system but it was not the nature of the economic system that triggered the invasion. In both cases, economic benefits may have accrued to the aggressor, but they were by-products, welcome payoffs, not causes.

The classic imperialist image of the private capitalist influencing policy for private gain does not adequately describe either the structure or motivation of United States policy.[14] The struggle to maintain an imperium, involving

14. Seymour Melman, *Pentagon Capitalism* (New York: McGraw-Hill, 1970), pp. 155–156. Melman presents the concept of "state-management" as a more fruitful analytic tool for explanation of U.S. policy: "The government of the United States now includes a self-expanding war machine that uses military power for diverse political operations and is based upon an industrial management that has priority claims to virtually unlimited capital funds from the federal budget. The state-management is economically parasitic, hence exploitative, in its relation to American society at home. The military-political operations of the Pentagon chieftains abroad, following the pattern of the Vietnam wars program, are parasitic there as well. To the older pattern of exploitative imperialism abroad there is now added an institutional network that is parasitic at home. This combina-

preparation for permanent warfare, the waging of war, the militarization of the economy and of society, has given precedence to politico-strategic motivations. Vietnam, then, demonstrates the interest of the governing class in maximizing its power on the world scene but it does not demonstrate the necessity of the policy in terms of the inner workings of the economic system. At most, it can be said that U.S. business interests follow the power train, and why not? Should U.S. functionaries have called in France or England to build hamlets and exploit newly discovered deposits of oil in Vietnam?

Vietnam is but one case, if a tragic one, but what about other areas? Hasn't the United States intervened to protect business interests in Latin America, Iran, and other countries? Hasn't intervention preserved corporate interests or assured the continued flow of oil with profits to American companies? This seems to have been true, but again, the economic motive is not primary in all cases and, at best, is intertwined with strategic factors. For example, Guatemala out of control may affect American business interests but it affects even more American domination of Central America. Hence the invasion of Guatemala to maintain the status quo, which does serve automatically to protect American business interests.

The economic explanation is too simple. To argue that aggression is in the nature of the system too often excludes political and psychological factors that are, in fact, in the nature of the system. Policy is a captive of the past operating in the framework of present exigencies. It was the particular circumstances of World War II that converted U.S.

---

tion is the new imperialism" (p. 34 and *passim*). See also Richard J. Barnet's discussion of "Military Socialism" in his *The Economy of Death* (New York: Atheneum, 1969). In connection with Melman's definition of state-management imperialism as exploitative of American society, see Juan Bosch's redefinition of imperialism as "pentagonism," distinguished by the imperialist country's exploitation, "colonizing," of its own people. (*Pentagonism, A Substitute for Imperialism*, tr. Helen R. Lane (New York: Grove Press, 1968), pp. 20–22.

isolationism into internationalism. The policies that it adopted were shaped by such traditional politico-military considerations as redefining power relationships and seeking advantage over the new challenger. Although the rehabilitation of western Europe may have been conceived as a vital factor in maintaining the health of the American economy over the long run, the Marshall Plan can hardly be squared with economic imperialism in the Leninist sense. And surely, the decision to make the defeated enemy the linchpin of American military policy in Europe is explainable in strategic rather than economic terms. Nevertheless, the particular policies the United States chose to pursue on the basis of its unparalleled military and economic power converted this country into an imperium that achieved direct and indirect control over the policies of many countries throughout the world. The taste of power led to the conscious pursuit of power by leaders who were convinced of the righteousness of their cause, the supremacy and virtue of the United States, and the wickedness of the enemy.

To conclude in this context with David S. Landes' rather transcendental definition: imperialism is "a multifarious response to a common opportunity that consists simply in disparity of power. Whenever and wherever such disparity has existed, people and groups have been ready to take advantage of it."[15] The inner logic of dominion consists of the fact that there is instability in any relationship of unequal power. Since the weaker power will not accept its inferiority, the stronger party must ceaselessly concern itself with the security of its position. In so doing, the imperial power assumes a spiral of increasing commitments and obligations that cannot be attributed primarily or basically to economic motives. So, Vietnam.

15. "Some Thoughts on the Nature of Economic Imperialism," *Journal of Economic History*, Vol. XXI, No. 4 (December 1961), pp. 496–512.

IV
The Neo-Realist
Theory of Imperialism

Unlike Marxist and Marxist-influenced writers, who have a ready-made theoretical framework to account for American policy, liberal writers have not treated critically and systematically the imperialist tendencies they noted in U.S. policy of the 1960's. One could speculate on the reasons for this: an ideological framework in which the United States and its policy have been regarded as progressive and, essentially, as justly reacting to the threat posed by Communism, thus dulling the edge of critical analysis; a psychological defense mechanism which militates against internalization of American atrocities visited on the population of Indochina; reluctance to accept the evidence that the United States has been recapitulating the unpleasant patterns of former imperial powers, etc. It is as if these writers regarded American policy as another "great aberration"[1] that will soon be corrected, returning us to sanctioned paths. Speculation aside, the many fine critical analyses of American policy did not offer an intellectual construct that comprehended the motive and dynamics of

1. In the manner of Samuel Flagg Bemis, commenting on the Spanish-American War and the acquisition of colonial possessions, in *A Diplomatic History of the United States*, 5th ed. (New York: Holt, Rinehart and Winston, 1965), pp. 463-75.

U.S. policy in the 1960's and that would consequently con-
tribute to an understanding of the future.

The outstanding exception to this, and one emanating
from a conservative scholar, is the theory developed by Dr.
George Liska, Professor in the International Studies Program of the Johns Hopkins University and research asso-
ciate at the Washington Center of Foreign Policy Research.
What makes his work deserving of special attention by
liberal and Marxist critics is his preoccupation with international political patterns that seem to recur throughout
history and his *de facto* rationalization of U.S. policy. As
repugnant as his views may be to a liberal or radical critic,
Liska's argument must be assessed carefully to test the validity of the critical view itself. In this vein, Liska's theory
of imperialism serves as counterpoint in the present essay
to the Marxist and radical view.

In his *Imperial America: The International Politics of
Primacy*[2] and the companion piece, *War and Order: Reflections on Vietnam and History*,[3] Liska views the emergence of the primacy of the United States on the world
scene as exemplifying a recurrent phenomenon in international relations. Much as Rome and England before it, the
United States has come of age, but in circumstances that
would define it as an "imperial," though not an "imperialist" or "imperialistic" power. That is, as Robert E. Osgood
comments in the foreword to the volume, the United
States, strikingly successful in its containment policy, im-
mensely powerful but of increasingly limited capacity for
direct control, will concern itself with fostering a tolerable
world order. "In a sense," Osgood writes, "the position of
the United States is analogous to that of an imperial though
nonimperialistic power." "Imperial" rather than "imperialist" apparently to place the United States within the
"grand" tradition of the empires of old, and to shield it

2. Baltimore: Johns Hopkins Press, 1967.
3. Baltimore: Johns Hopkins Press, 1968.

from the stigma associated with the label of "imperialism." Such semantic distinction cuts no ice tested against actual U.S. performance, which embraces economic exploitation, direct rule, indirect rule, and client states in addition to lofty purposes.

In contrast to the Marxist theory of imperialism, which proceeds from the dynamics of the given social system, Liska derives his theory from the conflicts and rivalries inherent in the game of international politics. That is, his analysis is derived essentially from external rather than internal factors. Imperialism is considered to be a function of certain laws deduced from the historical behavior of nation-states rather than a function of the capitalist system, as the Marxists would have it.[4] With its stress on power factors and on the external relations between the states, it might be called a "neo-realist"[5] theory of imperialism and international relations. Liska also stresses the responsibility and opportunity of power and the necessity of maintaining world order and stability. From this angle, Liska's theory represents the international counterpart to the domestic policy of "law and order": the "law and order theory of imperialism."

Liska's theory is a contemporary manifestation of the traditional approach to imperialism by historians and the "power-politics" school of international relations. Although domestic considerations are not excluded from the analysis, these scholars have tended to discount the economic factor, even in the acquisition of colonies in the

4. Curiously, Liska's analysis has an aura of historical determinism far beyond the Marxist, which stresses reciprocal internal and external factors. Historical determinism with a vengeance appears in another writer whose line of analysis is similar to—but not as sophisticated as—Liska's. Amaury de Riencourt's *The American Empire* (New York: Delta, 1970), self-described as "the study of the evolution of the United States imperial destiny as the Rome of the modern world—from its roots deep in the past to the troubled present and the preordained future" (p. xvii).

5. "Neo," to distinguish it from the "realist" school of international politics that came to oppose the "idealist" school after World War I.

nineteenth century. Rather, such scholars as William L. Langer[6] have emphasized nationalism, international rivalries, and political ambitions as the impetus for the acquisition of colonies and the European rivalries leading to World War I. The very nature of the nation-state system and the consequent pressure to increase, or at least maintain, power are, they wrote, major contributory factors to imperialist policy. These are the constant factors: in each historical period, there are additional variables that have to be factored in to account for the particular manifestation of the imperial phenomenon.

For Liska, as for many others, the official rationale for American involvement in Vietnam was unconvincing. Moreover, the critical literature on U.S. policy fell short of a compelling intellectual explanation of American involvement and its consequences. What Liska attempted to do instead was to place American policy in Vietnam in a broader theoretical perspective. Drawing on a rich historical background, and often arguing from historical analogy, he views the United States as having made it to the top through no particular design of its own but through the particular conflations of the international system. The United States has had the mantle of responsibility for world order thrust upon it by the constellation of world power that emerged after World War II. "In an unorganized world of conflicting and successive local and regional imperialisms," he writes in his preface, "the United States faces the imperial tasks of maintaining minimum order. . . ." The Vietnamese conflict will have to be understood and justified, not as a campaign to maintain the independence of a people or as the containment of Communism, but rather as a police operation that is inherent in America's world role. Until new global arrangements evolve, the

6. "A Critique of Imperialism," *Foreign Affairs*, Vol. XIV (October 1935), pp. 102–119, and *The Diplomacy of Imperialism, 1890–1902*, 2nd ed. (New York: Knopf, 1951).

U.S. war in Vietnam must be regarded as a necessary action which may well have to be repeated in order to secure American access to individual regions and to define the terms for the evolution of regional balances. This is a necessary role for the United States because, like the superstates of old—like the Roman Empire—it occupies a position of pre-eminent world power around which revolves the international political system.[7]

Liska rejects the model of bipolarity favored by international relations theorists during the 1960's because it implies an equality between the United States and the U.S.S.R. He does not, however, go so far as to posit a "unipolar" model, in deference, presumably, to the power of the U.S.S.R. Instead, he outlines a "unifocal" international political system on the ground that the policies of the various states revolve around their relation to the United States.[8] As *the* globally paramount power, the United States becomes automatically the power primarily responsible for shaping and maintaining a necessary modicum of world order.[9] One attribute follows from the other: paramount world power; responsibility for world order.

The United States achieved its pre-eminent position, according to Liska, with the aid of the "immemorial instruments of empire," to wit: "the wide diffusion, in friendly and dependent lands, of an American party [not further defined; presumably he means pro-American groups and

7. The comment in *The Pentagon Papers:* "But behind these foreign-policy axioms about domino effects, wars of liberation and the containment of China, the study reveals a deeper perception among the President [Johnson] and his aides that the United States was now the most powerful nation in the world and that the outcome in South Vietnam would demonstrate the will and the ability of the United States to have its way in world affairs.

"The study conveys an impression that the war was thus considered less important for what it meant to the South Vietnamese people than for what it meant to the position of the United States in the world." (New York: Bantam Books, 1971), p. 255.

8. *Alliances and the Third World* (Baltimore: Johns Hopkins Press, 1968), pp. 8–9.

9. *Imperial America,* p. 10.

political parties] . . . increasingly widespread economic ties converging at the center . . . and a military force, superior in both organization and key weapons to any other force in existence. . . ."[10] The United States' singular role as the imperial state in the unifocal international political system can be established in objective terms.

First, there is the "tendency for other states to be defined by their relation to the United States. . . ."[11] Presumably, this means that the political spectrum of nation-states derives its particular colors from the type of relationship each country has with the United States. A second key feature that defines the United States as the imperial power is "the great and growing margin for error in world affairs which guarantees that, barring an act of folly, the United States can do no wrong under the unwritten law of the balance of power. . . ."[12] Liska does not clarify this intriguing proposition. It could be interpreted as meaning that the imperial power does what it has to do to maintain world order as it sees fit and that it will not suffer any grievous consequences from its action, no matter what. (A less kindly interpretation would be that Liska is saying that the United States can get away with murder, which would accord very well with my characterization of his analysis as the "law and order theory of imperialism.") A third key feature of the system is a dialectical observation that the pre-eminence of American power is being redressed by the development of countervailing forces. In Liska's words, there is "the slow, hesitant, and still-inconclusive movement toward containment aimed at America's supremacy, which was wholly legitimately arrived at and largely beneficently exercised."[13]

Thus Liska's concept of the international political sys-

10. Ibid., p. 24.
11. Ibid., p. 26.
12. Ibid.
13. Ibid.

tem is not static. Although he describes the structure of world power as unifocal with the United States as its center, he sees in it the potentialities and characteristics of a multi-system. By this he means specifically that the given system contains within it the potential for the development of regional balance of power arrangements.

In Liska's model, the Soviet Union, the chief countervailing force to American power, would occupy the position of the foremost European power. Contrary to typical cold war analysts, Liska views the U.S.S.R. as a stabilizing force under certain stipulated conditions. He recognizes that it has reached a level of what is usually called responsibility and maturity that gives it a vested interest in maintaining the stability of Europe. But the U.S.S.R.'s role as the "foremost European power" presupposes the progressive reduction of U.S. political and economic involvement. The danger in this arrangement, of course, is the Soviet Union's military advantage vis-à-vis the European powers. This advantage would be neutralized, however, by the United States' maintaining its ultimate military security guarantee to the European states. Thus the stability of the area would be institutionalized in a European security pact built around the Soviet Union—and aimed implicitly at West Germany—but it would be circumscribed by the strategic vigilance of the United States as the condition of West Europe's self-confidence with regard to the U.S.S.R.

In contrast to the European scene, Liska argues that conditions are not yet propitious in other areas of the world for the creation of balances of power centered around other major powers. "Neither Latin America nor Africa has so far produced an indigenous regional power even remotely capable of doing more than fend for itself on a day-by-day basis."[14] And Latin America happens to be an area of special interest to the United States. Finally, in Asia, where China is attempting to achieve the role of primary power,

14. Ibid., pp. 81–82.

it has not acquired the "respectability" that the U.S.S.R. has, for example, in Europe. Therefore, here, as well as in Africa and Latin America, the United States will continue to bear the primary imperial responsibility. Regional arrangements, the balancing of power, remain the responsibility of the United States. In these areas, U.S. policy should have a dual characteristic, on the one hand directed toward fashioning a stable order and, at the same time, directed at a reduction of its responsibilities. This it can achieve by a judicious selection of economic aid, military-political alliances, and military intervention. In this mix, the economic instrument is downgraded. Liska is sceptical about the political payoff of economic instruments of policy, which take second place to the military in his scheme. Economic instruments of policy "are in themselves incapable of generating either a stable new order based on local responsibility or a sensible new attitude of responsiveness and reciprocity of recipients toward the chief donor."[15]

One of the conclusions he draws from this is the need for a "far-reaching professionalization of the military forces"[16] not only to make the military effective but also to insulate American society from the traumatic impacts of each and every peripheral involvement. Presumably, this is a generalization, drawn from the experience of Vietnam, which does not question the necessity of military action (there) but deplores the traumatic effect it has had on the American people. Imperial policy is, unfortunately, a problem for a democratic polity which sooner or later comes to subject the policies of its leaders to critical scrutiny.

This summary does not do justice to Liska's erudition or to the nuances of his argument, but it is intended to be a fair rendition of his conception of America's role in world affairs. It is, moreover, not an entirely unpersuasive model of "imperial America." If, as Liska's presentation seems to

15. Ibid., p. 84.
16. Ibid., p. 106.

ask, one could just shed the emotional reaction to the Vietnam war and view U.S. policy in Vietnam as only one, albeit a highly critical, instance of U.S. policy as it has developed after World War II—if one could view policy in cold blood—one could comprehend the forces behind U.S. behavior. Whether one likes it or not is another matter. In fact, critics would do well to take Liska's model seriously, for it rubs in a world outlook much like that of Nixon's foreign affairs adviser, Henry Kissinger, and represents an able presentation of a traditional point of view. And that may be its major failing.

What Liska does—and what the so-called realistic theorist of international relations does—is to take what is as given and project upon it. What is given is the anarchical structure of international society and the historically verifiable fact that states use their power to their own best advantage in this "vacuum." What matters is power. Those who have it will—and must—exercise it in more or less traditional ways to provide an international environment congenial to their own prosperity. At least, they will exercise power to avoid unsettling conflict in order to maintain what they have.[17] Empire and imperialism have always been a feature of this exercise of power; the present period is no exception, even though the particular motives and forms of action may differ. If there is a weakness in Liska's theory of imperium, it is, however, precisely in its mode of analysis.

Derivation of theory from the verities of international politics suffers at least two major weaknesses. First, it tends to project patterns of the past into the present without due allowance for significant alterations in the military, economic, and political setting. True, there is a tendency to fill power vacuums, for Great Powers to seek absolute

17. Or, in Liska's terminology, "access to local balances or hierarchies of power and influence . . . the irreducible object of the statecraft of an imperial power." *War and Order*, pp. 66–67.

rather than relative advantage, and relative advantage rather than no advantage, and for combinations of powers to offset the power of a dominant state. Yet the historical analogy of Rome may be more misleading than suggestive because of qualitative changes in the international scene. Obviously, the availability of nuclear weapons has affected the means of implementing policy, and hence the policy itself. The employment of nuclear weapons to finish off North Vietnam or to "neutralize" China did not appear to be a serious possibility. Moreover, the differences between the Powers, especially between the Great Powers, need not result in policies that would validate the recapitulation of old patterns of action.[18] Economic competition between leading capitalist powers need not result in war, if only because of the disparities of power. Associations of states to regulate competition may have lasting political and economic effects. As relations between the U.S.S.R. and the United States reveal, even the ideologically hostile superpowers have more in common than at issue. For that matter, the United States does not have problems with the Soviet Union—or with China, the Germanies, or Japan—that would require it to pursue an aggressive aggrandizing policy, if only international issues were at stake.

I am not arguing that conflicts, even serious ones, do not exist between the United States and other states. I am contending, however, that the nature of these problems in this particular historical period may have outcomes contrary to the patterns of the past, and that the essential one-dimensionality of Liska's analysis neglects to a fault both the domestic political and economic factors that affect U.S. pol-

18. Academicians and textbook authors on international politics tend to reify historical patterns of action rather than appraise the possibilities for a "breakthrough into the present" which may offer the basis for new patterns of action. College youth do resist the historical dimension because it suggests limitations on human action but at the same time they are aware that the historical dimension serves to inhibit new departures and conserve what seem to be irrational forms of behavior.

icy. President Nixon's Canossa to Peking, which implied the liquidation of the Taiwan policy, demonstrates how contrived U.S. policy has been and illustrates the importance of the manipulative and domestic political aspects of U.S. foreign policy. After all, the American war in Indochina was justified as a necessary measure to contain the People's Republic of China, as was American support of Taiwan. What changed was not the policy of China with regard to its outlying areas but the attitude of Nixon, who now adopted the view of those whom he had been assailing for years without, however, providing any justification different from theirs.

The neo-realist line of analysis by analogy is also deficient in failing to draw distinctions between the specific characteristics of particular socio-political systems at particular points in history. Although I have downgraded economics as the motor of imperialist policy in Lenin's terms, economic factors have influenced policy, and still do. Similarly, the type of political system may also influence foreign policy decisions; the neo-realist analysis fails to take this sufficiently into account and falls into the trap of direct historical analogy. For example, the fact that noncapitalist empires and imperiums have existed does not rule out the possibility that capitalist imperialisms with their own specific features may be motivated by different considerations. If the export of capital was a nonexistent consideration in Roman imperialism, this does not rule out the possibility that the export of capital (and organizational technique) is one of the driving forces of American imperialism. If businessmen were despised in Rome, this does not mean that American businessmen are not influential in the formulation of foreign policy.

From another angle, if the masses in the Roman or British Empire had little to say in the formulation of foreign policy, it does not follow that the American people have no influence over foreign policy (though the deep-rooted tendency of the American people to trust their leaders in this realm because "they know better" is cause for despair). The course of the Vietnam war shows that the American people have, at least, a tempering influence on policy. There *is* something to the cliché that totalitarian regimes—and kingdoms and oligarchies—are far less hampered in the conduct of their foreign policy than democracies.

Liska is certainly not unaware of domestic considerations, but his failure to analyze both the influence of the economic structure on U.S. policy and domestic political pressures is a serious omission in attempting to delineate the driving forces of American international behavior. For example, when he argues that the United States has achieved its pre-eminent position through, among others, "increasingly widespread economic ties converging at the center,"[19] what is he pointing to except the operations of American capitalism abroad? But he makes no connection between the economic activity and the nature of the policy pursued by the United States. Indeed, he would do well to incorporate the Marxist analysis, which shows the importance of American policy abroad and its ties with the "center." It would certainly provide a more substantial infrastructure for his argument, the difference with the Marxists being that Liska would preserve, and the Marxists change, the system. As regards the input of the American masses into policy, Liska is wary and seemingly against it. His statement that the American people should be shielded from the traumatic effects of necessary foreign interventions[20] implies that a "rational imperial" policy can be conducted only by "steely-eyed statesmen," as someone once remarked.

It is not difficult to find flaws in Liska's analysis, but the importance of his *Imperial America* is not so much the analysis as it is the function his theory serves. As a frame-

19. See above, pp. 44–5.
20. See above, p. 47.

work for American involvement in Vietnam, it justifies the interventionist role of the United States in world affairs as a necessary part of a policy aimed at establishing and maintaining world order and stability. American initiative and action are required to provide the appropriate world setting for the maintenance of the American position. It is a conservative doctrine that allows for modulated change occurring through established frameworks. It will maintain American primacy in the foreseeable future; over the long run, presumably the United States will suffer the fate of other imperiums. In contrast to the Marxist theory of imperialism and revolution, Liska's theory may with some license be called a theory of imperialism and counterrevolution. At home, the theory implies the maintenance of the corporate structure, stability, and discipline. It implies domestic adjustments to foreign policy, not the other way around.[21] Liska provides a convenient framework for the Nixonian phase of American imperialism—the culmination of liberal Democratic policy —which has introduced repressive action to maintain domestic "law and order" while it maintains "world order and stability."

21. One of Liska's startling examples of the interrelationship of domestic and foreign policy is the "interdependence" he sees between the assertion of U.S. power in Vietnam and the "prospect for a semi-orderly integration of American society in the face of Black Power." The inability of the United States to carry out its imperial role successfully, he thinks, might very well result in a "Second American Revolution" for the independence of this hitherto colonized group, that is a Black revolution on the order of 1776, or 1905 or 1917 in Russia! *War and Order, op. cit.*, pp. 87–88.

V

By Way of Conclusion

What, after all, is the function of theory? It is, most simply stated, to stipulate the probability of the occurrence of an event under certain conditions. When conditions have changed, Marxists in the past have revised their ideas, countering certain tenets advanced by Marx, but nevertheless maintaining their faith in the Marxist mode of analysis. Both Lenin and Bernstein, for example, in setting diametrically opposed courses, revolutionary and evolutionary socialism respectively, claimed to do so in the name of Marx. More to the point is what they saw to be inoperative in Marx's schema and the need to provide new guidelines to the socialist and working-class movement.

Thus, Lenin's theory of imperialism was an implicit admission that Marx's theory of revolution was invalid. Exploitation and alienation of the proletariat, polarization of the classes, and revolutionary consciousness were the necessary preconditions for revolution. Yet history simply had not borne out Marx's reasoning that under the intensive exploitation of the capitalist system, the proletariat would develop a revolutionary consciousness and move to seize power. Lenin attempted to shore up Marx's theory by introducing a qualitatively new factor—capitalism's external operations—which, on the one hand, was represented as having slowed down the revolutionary process as envisioned by Marx, but, on the other, as providing the catalyst for revolution—that is, imperialist conflict. But just as Lenin recognized that Marx's analysis had been outstripped by events, so has Lenin's analysis been vitiated by history. Imperialist conflict did not cause revolution in any advanced capitalist society. It was an important contextual fact with regard to the Russian revolution but no more than that. There may be a theoretical explanation of revolutions that did occur in certain countries, but it is not the traditional Marxist or Leninist theory of revolution.

The Marxist-Leninist theory of capitalist (and socialist) foreign policy is similarly open to doubt. Central to the theory is the notion that the nature of the socio-economic system determines the character of foreign policy. Hence, capitalism, in its search for profits, must operate outside its national borders, enmeshing other countries in its exploitative techniques and automatically involving the protective apparatus of state power. In contrast, socialist countries, by definition, are not so engaged. Their foreign policy is directed to the protection and perfection of the socialist system, which requires peace and tranquillity abroad. Now, there is no dispute that capitalism is an international phenomenon and that capitalism is specific to American imperialism, but it does not necessarily follow that American policy is determined by capitalism's foreign interests.[1] There is here, concededly, a partial explanation of policy. But what Marxists have not come to grips with, to mention a few major points, is that the capitalist enterprise is involved largely with the advanced capitalist countries—not the underdeveloped countries; that the internal mechanisms which Marx, Lenin, and others predicted would de-

[1] ". . . although imperialism is a function of economic expansion, it is not a necessary function. Whether imperialist phenomena show themselves or not, is determined not only by the factors of economic expansion, but equally by the political and social organization of the regions brought into the orbit of the expansive society, and also by the world situation in general." John Gallagher and Ronald Robinson, "The Imperialism of Free Trade," *Imperialism and Colonialism*, George H. Nadel and Perry Curtis, eds. (New York: Macmillan, 1964), p. 102.

velop to oppose the capitalists simply failed to materialize; and finally, they have failed to face up squarely to the constrictions placed on any ruling group by the structure of the nation-state system.

If we follow along the Marxist-Leninist theory for the sake of argument, the overturn of the capitalist order would install a "socialist" government in power. Now, it is not at all clear what form a socialist society in the United States would take. The only guidelines available are those derived from self-styled socialist governments that took power in backward areas. But, in general terms, nationalization of the means of production would be on the agenda (Marx's public ownership), corporate wealth would be channeled into public funds, gross disparities of individual wealth would disappear, social services would increase, and the government would be placed in the hands of socially-minded groups by fiat or perhaps through democratic process. Even without a blueprint for the future, such a development might well be an improvement over what exists. But what of foreign affairs? What evidence or indication is there that a socialist government would behave, or could behave, much differently from a capitalist government?

Surely, one could argue that a socialist government would be directed toward peace and welfare and a less exploitative economic policy in the underdeveloped countries. But how much freedom of action would a socialist government have? Would socialized corporate enterprise be employed overseas much differently under socialism? Again, there is little guidance from the past because socialist revolutions have taken place in countries that were not internationally powerful, at least during and immediately after the revolution. The initial driving force, in international affairs, was to build power, ostensibly for purposes of survival in the face of capitalist threat. But beyond this, the record of behavior of the U.S.S.R. and the People's Republic of China (which many will not term "socialist" anyway) gives little indication that they have broken out of the entrapment of the international system. The conduct of the socialist countries in foreign affairs is of a piece with that of the capitalists. Even if the replacement of despotic backward regimes by revolutionary socialist governments is regarded as a progressive development, the foreign policy of the socialist governments has moved in traditional patterns, even to the point of socialist countries' exploiting and threatening each other. What evidence is there that the multiplication of socialist states would alter the pattern drastically?

There is little comfort in the rationale that the revolution was betrayed by Stalin and his epigones, that if the revolutionaries had remained true to their Marxist socialist principles, things would have been different. Even those who once looked to China to redeem revolutionary Marxism now feel themselves betrayed by its accommodation with the United States and the capitalist countries. Nor is there much solace in Trotsky's theory of permanent revolution, which has a vogue among those radicals who feel that the Communist parties have sold out. One may agree with Trotsky that modern capitalism, in forging the interdependence of mankind, has, perforce, rendered the nation-state obsolete and that the agenda calls for socialist revolution, which would rationalize economic problems and substitute an international socialist community for the system of states as it now exists. But how to break through the realities to install a "rational" international order? Marxist theory may provide a sane and moral prospectus; it provides little in the way of operational politics. The Marxist-Leninist theory of imperialism and revolution is dated. One of its chief deficiencies is its economic thrust—the relative lack of weight it assigns to political factors in governing policy and change, as suggested in Chapter II.

In the conduct of American foreign policy, it appears that political factors have come to outweigh economic factors. These overriding political factors are both international and domestic. Internationally, the world is composed of nation-states which are constantly jockeying for position, whether it is to maintain the status quo or to achieve advantage through various means, including force of arms. In this international system of states, the Great Powers, separately or in concert as the situation warrants, attempt to arrange matters to suit their convenience. This has been the conscious thrust of U.S. foreign policy evidenced in Franklin D. Roosevelt's idea of a post-World-War-II peace enforced by the Great Powers, now revived by Richard M. Nixon's new Metternichean policy.

The compelling domestic political factor is a more or less homogeneous governing group in the United States that has convinced itself of the virtue of the American way, the need for military superiority, and the maintenance, so far as possible, of the international status quo. This posture is not merely the product of private economic interest but also the consequence of the bureaucratization of the civilian and military establishment enforced by the ideological brainwashing of the American public. The idea of what the United States is and how it must behave in the international arena is so firmly ingrained that change indeed seems almost impossible. After ten years of absent-minded genocide in Vietnam, race riots, massive student protest, and unemployment and inflation in the American polity, the challengers of policy offer no more than a reduction of the military budget, while they conform to the essential lines of U.S. foreign policy, and domestically hold out the possibility of tax reform. It is as if nothing has been learned[2], or if it has, the lesson cannot be implemented be-

2. Take, for example, the "dean" of American scholars of international politics, Hans J. Morgenthau, who still can write that in addition to its primary national interest—the security of its territory and institutions—

cause of the rigidities in the domestic and international structure.

The notion of political leaders being "captured" cannot be lightly dismissed. I would argue that the political leaders of the Great Powers must gamble to bring foreign policy more nearly in line with the realities of the times. The United States had the opportunity to do so in the 1950's when its power was unmatched. A unilateral decision to halt the development of A and H bombs and the reduction of armaments might well have influenced other states in the same direction. Risky, yes. But is it more risky and less acceptable than living as we do, saddled with stupendous military budgets, placing our faith in the "delicate balance of terror" to insure our security and well-being?

Assuming that political leaders of the Great Powers are not guided by a death wish—an assumption that does not come easily—the revolution in weaponry has made war obsolete as an instrument of policy between Great Powers. This, in itself, would have rationally required a revision in the rules of the game of international politics. But even under the old rules, the existing U.S. arsenal is more than sufficient to insure the national security, the physical security of the United States. The country needs less, not more. The problem of security is psychological rather than military. Increasing military strength does not necessarily improve national security; in some cases it is even meaningless. The political factor is emerging as a more significant one in creating areas of security—the structuring of

---

"the United States has a number of secondary interests in the world, such as peace and security everywhere, the protection and promotion of democratic governments, the containment of Communist governments and movements, the relief of poverty and disease. . . .

"The security of the United States is today threatened not only in the traditional way by hegemonial powers in Europe and Asia . . . but also by the exposure of the American territory to nuclear destruction . . . and by the exposure of American institutions to ideological competition and subversion from abroad. . . ." *A New Foreign Policy for the United States* (New York: Praeger, 1969), pp. 241–242.

international political arrangements accompanied by arms reduction and control. The trend is not toward replicating old-style collective security systems, but toward transforming the present security arrangements into substantially new forms.[3] No one threatens the security of the United States. (When is this ever going to permeate the consciousness of Americans?) The problem is one of national insecurity perpetrated by the leaders, opinion-makers, and politicians of this country,[4] (and of others, it must be said). A drastic reorientation of the notion of "defense" is required by the very changes that have taken place in weaponry.

The usual rebuttal to this contention is that national security cannot be equated with physical security; the notion of physical security is too narrow. Security consists not only of physical inviolability but of a world that is friendly or at least not hostile, that will buy your goods and sell you whatever you want. Even if the physical security of the United States is not in jeopardy, it is alleged that it is necessary to maintain a large and technically up-to-date military establishment to be employed as an instrument of policy. It is necessary, for example, to insure that governments do not fall into unfriendly (a euphemism generally for Communist) hands in order to preserve American security —more generally conceived, to insure the inflow of vital products and raw materials.

Yet this contention is not supported by the evidence. A country that falls to the Communists does not automatically deprive the United States of accustomed materials. Rather, what has occurred is that the United States has imposed restrictions on trade with such countries. A country,

3. See Ljubivoje Aćimović's "Military Aspects of European Security," International Colloquy on Military Aspects of European Security, Belgrade, December 15–16, 1972 (Belgrade: Institute of International Politics and Economics, 1972).

4. One of the more challenging analyses of national security is Samuel L. Sharp's "Security and Threatmanship," *America's World Role in the 70's*, ed. Abdul A. Said (Englewood Cliffs, N.J.: Prentice-Hall-Spectrum 1970), pp. 30–42.

capitalist or Communist, will sell the products it cannot consume. A Communist country is not an autarkic country. The more industrialized it becomes, the more sophisticated and varied its products, the greater its interest in international trade. Underdeveloped countries, those dependent on one or two basic crops, are even more at the mercy of the foreign market. They may nationalize industries but they still have to sell. Nationalization certainly cuts into the profits of American enterprise, but the right of a country to control its own enterprise cannot be denied. The extension of sovereignty in the former colonial areas argues for the nationalization of foreign enterprise, which may be considered a progressive and healthy step toward a readjustment of the way in which these less affluent countries deal with their capitalist and socialist neighbors. The cost of pursuing an imperialist policy in Vietnam may be driving a lesson home. Although the interventionist reflexes of corporate enterprise and public policy were manifest in a desire to abort the Marxist-led government of Chile, yet official American counter-action to nationalization was feeble. Perhaps the business community will come to the realization that intervention outweighs the benefits and that profits are still to be had through other forms of international corporate enterprise.

If Marxist theories of imperialism have failed to deal adequately with international and domestic factors, as argued above, so the realist theory of imperialism has failed to grasp the changing nature of the international order and has neglected the domestic components of policy. Liska's position is that the United States must continue to play an intelligent imperial role or suffer the historically inevitable decline and fall of empire. In Liska's rationale, the failure of U.S. policy in Vietnam does not invalidate his theory. Rather, it would be ascribed to a failure of nerve, to the weakness of American leadership in doing what would have to be done domestically and internationally to achieve its objectives. Domestic policy would have to be bent to support the imperial mission: a conservative, law-and-order society would be the required underpinning of intelligent imperial policy. Assuming that such a society is not distasteful to Liska, he does not, however, explain the widespread disaffection in the United States and the loss of faith of the American people in the credibility of its political leadership. Perhaps his conclusion would be that the leadership has failed in its mission and the United States, like Rome, is headed for a decline. Are the students the modern version of the barbarian hordes?

Marxist and traditional critics, after all, represent only a small fraction of the critics of U.S. foreign policy. The largest, most vociferous challenge to American policy—to its imperialism—has come from the liberals, who, nevertheless, have not produced substantially innovative guidelines for foreign or domestic policy. These liberal critics—the "limitationists" and "neo-isolationists"—could be said to share a Hobsonian notion that imperialism is not an inexorable function of capitalism, that capitalism is, so to speak, autonomous in the choice of its foreign policy. Hobson identified the "taproot of imperialism"[5] as the excess of production over domestic consumption—hence the need to find foreign markets. It followed that the remedy was to raise domestic consumption so that there would be only a modest surplus to be traded off abroad, thus undercutting the roots that lead to the growth of the imperialist complex.

The Hobsonian model is appealing, translated into contemporary terms: domestic investment to eradicate poverty, establishment of a floor for minimum living standards, more generous allocation of resources to cope with environmental problems, etc., etc., instead of massive foreign investment, huge military budgets—and imperial in-

5. J. A. Hobson, *Imperialism, A Study* (London: Allen & Unwin, 1948), pp. 80–81.

volvement. Yet the Hobsonian model is too simple both in terms of the contemporary structure of capitalism and of the international political system and the domestic political structure. How does one change the minds of a governing class that is caught up in its idea of American economic and political dominance?

Hobson's position is too "rational," much like Schumpeter's,[6] which sees imperialism as an "atavism" impeding the development of an interdependent and peaceful world through the medium of capitalism. The liberal critics, more cognizant perhaps of political factors, simply call for more "rational" goals for American policy. They trust that the United States would profit if it set itself more modest goals, implying that matters would improve domestically as a consequence. Their view is, perhaps, post-Hubert H. Humphrey (all to the good), but there is very little specific, let alone radical, in what they have to suggest on policy. As one commentator has put it:

> What, after all, is the meaning of limitationism other than what the term itself implies: that there are limits to a nation's, any nation's, power and that these limits must in turn set limits to a nation's interests and purposes. The principle is unexceptionable as a counsel of prudence. . . . At the same time, it need not prove incompatible with an expansionist and imperial outlook.[7]

Stanley Hoffman, in a telling criticism of the balance of power strategy implicit in the Nixon-Kissinger policies, asks the rhetorical question: "Does it not rather reflect our hope to preserve our past eminence . although at bargain prices?"[8]

6. Joseph A. Schumpeter, *Imperialism and Social Classes* (New York: Meridian Books, 1955).

7. Robert W. Tucker, *The Radical Left and American Foreign Policy*, p. 5. See also pp. 97 ff. for his discussion of "security."

8. "Weighing the Balance of Power," *Foreign Affairs*, Vol. 50, No. 4 (July 1972), p. 641.

Let us not [he concludes] confuse a set of worthy goals—the establishment of a moderate international system, new relations with our adversaries, the adjustment of our alliances to the new conditions of diplomacy and economics—with a technique—a balance of five powers—that turns out to correspond neither to the world's complex needs nor to our own ambivalent desires. A "structure of peace" cannot be brought about by restoring a bygone world. Rediscovering the "habits of moderation and compromise" requires a huge effort of imagination and innovation.[9]

Unfortunately the "breakthrough" Hoffman is looking for, which transcends the Nixon-Kissinger "breakthrough," requires more of the imagination of an R. D. Laing than that of the conventional theorist of international politics.

Whatever considerable service the critics of American policy have performed, they have not, then, articulated guidelines for significant change. Policy may be shorn of its anti-Communist virulence, and interventions on the scale of Indochina may be a thing of the past, but policy will be conducted pretty much as in the past, and the policy-making group will remain the same. Incremental progress? Good! But nothing more?

From a period of isolationism—or "unilateralism," as some prefer—American policy moved from containment (limited commitment) to globalism and was tripped up on the war in Vietnam. With American consensus turning into opposition to the war, there has, nevertheless, not developed any coherent idea of what U.S. policy should be. For all the conservative-liberal, liberal-conservative, liberal-realist, or what-have-you criticism of the conduct of the war, the unmistakable impression is that those in the influential positions of policymaker, politician, journalist, or academician have little else to offer than the counsel of choosing wiser policies and exercising greater political in-

9. Ibid., p. 643.

telligence. They are variously critical of policy influenced by frozen ideological sets, anti-Communism, anti-radicalism, overcommitment, etc., but they offer neither an alternate concept of national security (except to criticize official versions), nor do they explicitly lay out the means that would be employed to pursue the type of policy they prefer.

In short, they are just as much caught up in the given frame of reference as the policy-makers and their articulators. Perhaps they would exercise their options more wisely; perhaps they would have cut out of Vietnam earlier or never have become involved, and perhaps the normalization of relations with China would have commenced earlier. And no doubt that is better than we have had it and perhaps that is all we can expect. But it hardly signifies a substantial shift in policy and in the allocation of priorities and resources.

If there were any doubt about this, the reaction to the Administration's policies should dispel it. President Nixon's moves in 1970 and 1971 to scale down the war in Vietnam, pursue accommodation with the U.S.S.R., repair the break with China, and shore up the domestic economy were sufficient to take the steam out of the antiwar movement, neutralize much of liberal criticism, and even get him support on a domestic program that was on the face of it favorable to big business and the wealthy at the expense of the wage earners and salariat. And even given the horror of the war in Vietnam and the divisive tendencies that ripped out in the open in the sixties, neither major political party offers a prospectus of significant change. The body politic is centrist with a list to one side or other. The Republican and Democratic parties may be conceived of as a single conservative body with leanings to the left and right. There is little to distinguish Hubert H. Humphrey's ideas on foreign policy from Nixon's except that Nixon is a less inhibited innovator. The body politic wanted the war in Indochina ended because it had not been brought to a successful conclusion, but it is most concerned with maintaining the status quo, stability; it is reacting against the upheavals of the 1960's, the threat of the underprivileged and disaffected, the open violence in the society, and the prospect of changes in policy that would affect middle-class economic well-being. Not only are the "middle Americans" hostile to radical tendencies, they are fearful of rocking the boat of plenty as represented in the mildly reformist campaign of George McGovern.

If the Marxist-Leninist theory of imperialism is inadequate to the times, it does not follow that all Marxist ideas and a Marxist mode of analysis are therefore unuseful. Marxists seem to agree (but only Marxists?) that policy is made by a privileged, fairly homogeneous economic and social elite supported by entrenched bureaucracies which may have their own career interests to pursue but operate within the framework of the elite's value system. It is this power elite that has to be replaced, but how? Through what mechanisms? How can radical dissent be sustained and translated into effective action? It must be recognized, first of all, how effectively dissent is coordinated and absorbed by the "system."[10] A new program, a new federal bureau—palliatives. Today's dissent becomes tomorrow's fashion, usually with a commercial profit attached to it. Moreover, the governmental apparatus disposes of overwhelming military and police forces, which make the possibility of direct action to seize power virtually impossible. The system does produce its own antagonists—blacks, students, the radical poor—but in no way do they constitute a class in the Marxist sense and, more important, they do not share the concerns that would weld them into an effective oppositional force—Marx's revolutionary instrument.

Marcuse's appeal to the New Left consisted in part of his break with ritualized Marxism, his rejection of the concept

10. Herbert Marcuse, *One-Dimensional Man* (Boston: Beacon, 1964).

of the revolutionary proletariat and of the organic transformation of capitalism into socialism. Instead he wrote of
the need for a sharp break with the present order, for the
purpose of creating the preconditions for a "free" society,
a society of radical sensibility in which the release of libidi-
nal energy would be made possible in a new institutional
framework. Marcuse's unique reinterpretation of Freud
and Marx appealed to the youth in its elucidation of the
possibilities of a freer life style in a new social order. But
it was mistaken to view Marcuse as a revolutionary theorist equipped with an operational political strategy. He is
rather a philosopher of revolution, holding out the possibilities of freedom, of a socialist humanism in the Hege-
lian-Marxist tradition. He never saw revolution on the
agenda, though he may have been excited by the possibilities uncovered in the 1960's; he even denied that society
was in a prerevolutionary situation. Hence the disenchant-
ment with Marcuse of many young activists. Marcuse was
fully aware of the stabilizing and counter-progressive factors in American society and his writing consistently warns
of regressive tendencies even as he outlines the possibilities
for "liberation." He is a philosopher of hope tinged with
deep pessimism and at times despair.[11]

If the traditional Marxist theory of revolution and the
Marxist-Leninist theory of imperialism are rejected as in-
appropriate for an advanced industrial society, what then
in Marxism remains useful as a guideline for change? Basic
would appear to be the fundamental idea of contradiction
between the forces of production and the relations of production, or in plainer English, the idea that industrial,
technological, and scientific development is rendering obsolete existing forms of social organization and capitalist

11. Or so it seems to me. Bibliographies of Marcuse's work appear in *The
Critical Spirit, Essays in Honor of Herbert Marcuse*, ed. Kurt H. Wolff and
Barrington Moore, Jr. (Boston: Beacon, 1967), and in Robert W. Marks,
The Meaning of Marcuse (New York: Ballantine Books, 1970). Marcuse's
most recent book is *Counter-Revolution and Revolt* (Boston: Beacon, 1972).

values and, thereby, creating the conditions for a freer, more equitable humane society (and also, it must be stressed, the possibilities of an even more coordinated and repressed society). The idea of a qualitatively different way of life in "post-industrial society," already foreshadowed in contemporary America, is no monopoly of Marxists. Borrowing from Servan-Schreiber's eloquent statement:

> There is a new society on the horizon, one which will come into being before today's 30-year-olds go into retirement. Not only will it be a richer society, but a different kind of society, since beyond a certain level wealth is measured not so much by a higher standard of living as a completely different way of life. The "post-industrial society" will be distinguished by man's unprecedented freedom from physical, economic, and biological constraints. Manual labor will have virtually disappeared, there will be more leisure time than hours of work, distance will be annihilated, spectacular new methods for the diffusion of culture and information will be developed, and we will enjoy a vastly increased new power over nature and life. Will this be a happier society? That is a different question to which we have no answer. But it is certain that this society will form the avant-garde of human history, and that concerns us.[12]

And it does appear that the New Left of the 1960's was the avant-garde that reflected the changing nature and values of American society. Assuming possibilties for change in a radical direction, how is it going to come about and who (what groups, classes?) represents the instrument of change?

We may as well face up to the fact that our political tools of analysis are woefully inadequate for tackling these questions. When we get down to cases, it is no easy matter to demonstrate in a convincing way what individuals or groups actually manage foreign policy, their mode of operation, the interrelationships between domestic and for-

12. Servan-Schreiber, *The American Challenge*, p. 65.

eign concerns.[13] We may have an idea of the changes we would like to see, changes that *seem* possible within the society, yet the dynamics of change, the forces making for change, and the direction of change are most difficult to analyze. Marxists generally consider the development of a political consciousness the necessary precondition for radical change. It is the one Marxian concept that has retained its force even among the elitist persuasion of Marxists who rely more on the inculcation of consciousness "from above" than on its organic development through "praxis," through thought and action. Marcuse's recent works may be read as an effort in enlightenment, in the consciousness-raising that is indispensable to radical change.

But it is not only Marxists who see the development of a new political consciousness as the key to change in America. Charles A. Reich's *The Greening of America*[14] was an easy mark for the critics; yet his essential point is that there is observably a new consciousness growing out of the experience of the new generation that has the potential of changing the value structure of America. It is true that Reich's Yale students represent a select and privileged segment of the new generation whose values and aspirations may be far from those of a ghetto youth or a down-state Hoosier student. Yet they do reflect changes that have come about in upper-middle-class America and the disaffection appears throughout the student movement, and not only the student movement.

The student movement of the 1960's, maturing in the madness of the Indochinese war, was a catalyst for challenge to the established order. But if it were a matter only

13. Norman Birnbaum, "The Crisis in Marxist Sociology," *Social Research*, Vol. 35, No. 2 (Summer 1968) pp. 348–380, especially pp. 364–366.

14. New York: Random House, 1970. A collection of critical essays appears in *The Con III Controversy*, edited by Philip Nobile (New York: Pocket Books, 1971). See Reich's articles in the *New York Times*, March 8, 1971, p. 31, and March 9, 1971, p. 35, in which he defends his idea of "revolution by consciousness" and mildly puts down those critics who had accused him of a facile glorification of the youth culture.

of student discontent, prompted by the threat of physical destruction in a war the purpose of which seemed obscure, it could have been written off as a particular manifestation of a regularly-occurring generation gap. But this was not the case, for the protest movement brought into the open more general discontent with American society: the powerlessness of the individual in a formal democracy ("participatory democracy"), racial inequality (S.N.C.C. and others), the routinized and repressed existence of the middle class who had made it (the "counter-culture"), the irrational and destructive use of American wealth and power (the antiwar movement), etc. That the students had hit upon a tender nerve exposing the discontents of the middle class itself was evident from the often hysterical reaction to student protest and, as Arthur Miller, I think it was, observed, the actual hatred that developed between father and son (certainly evident on the campus).

The student movement peaked in the Kent-Cambodia crisis and, in frustration at its evident powerlessness to affect policy, went underground. The press and other commentators, obviously relieved, talked and wrote about the students' return to their studies, a contracting job market that was placing pressure on students to work harder and to compete more actively (just like the good old days of the 1930's?). But the students are still there and it is true that they will grow older and take their places in society but perhaps this is not as comforting a thought as it appears. For the traditional value structure is already broken down among the students—and not only the college students.[15] They, and the high school students who will occupy their desks, are more sceptical and critical than the students who matriculated in 1960. They will indeed fill the positions for which society has trained them but the open question

15. Philip Slater writes perceptively of the continuities and discontinuities between the old and new culture in *The Pursuit of Loneliness* (Boston: Beacon, 1970), pp. 108–109 and *passim*.

is will they do so in the same spirit as their elders. They may have grown up less absurd and their children perhaps even less so.

In his *Greening*, Reich wrote that "the theory of revolution by consciousness appears to run squarely contrary to the teaching of Marx that the structure of society is maintained by the privileged or ruling classes for their own benefit, and hence cannot be changed except by a revolution which attacks the power of rulers."[16] Reich recognizes that the development of a political consciousness was central to Marx's thought; what he is counterposing to Marx is his notion of revolution through persuasion rather than forcible seizure of power. Although Reich's "yeast theory of revolution"[17]—the new generation must spread its life-style—is easily ridiculed, there is something to the idea of the permeation of new ideas, values, and styles to effect changes, if not "revolution," in American society. Something of the sort is going on now: women's lib and the legalization of abortion are nothing if not a rejection of bourgeois capitalist norms. What is also at stake is the translation of new values into institutional forms, into an organized political movement that will view the world, and America's role in it, somewhat differently. For with all due consideration of historical experience and extant theories of politics (and theories of imperialism), the rapid transformation of our world since World War II calls for a reordering of our own society and of our attitudes and policies toward the rest of the world.

16. *The Greening of America*, p. 322.
17. Ibid., p. 321.

Selected Bibliography

Aguilar, Alonso. *Pan-Americanism, From Monroe to the Present*, tr. Asa Zats. New York: Monthly Review Press, 1968.

Arendt, Hannah. *The Origins of Totalitarianism*. New York: Harcourt, Brace, 1951. Part Two, *Imperialism*, was published separately as a Harvest paperback.

Arnold, G. L. (pseudonym, George Lichtheim). "The Imperial Impact on Backward Countries." *St. Antony's Papers*, No. 2, pp. 104–125. See also Lichtheim, George.

Baran, Paul A. *The Political Economy of Growth*. New York: Monthly Review Press, 1957.

——, and Sweezy, Paul M. *Monopoly Capital, An Essay on the American Economic and Social Order*. New York and London: Monthly Review Press, 1966.

Barnet, Richard J. *Intervention and Revolution*. Cleveland and New York: World (Meridian Books), 1969.

——. *The Economy of Death*. New York: Atheneum, 1969.

Bemis, Samuel Flagg. *Diplomatic History of the United States*, 5th ed. New York: Holt, Rinehart and Winston, 1965.

Bernstein, Eduard. *Evolutionary Socialism*, tr. Edith C. Harvey. New York: Schocken, 1961.

Birnbaum, Norman. "The Crisis in Marxist Sociology," *Social Research*, Vol. 35, No. 2 (Summer 1968), pp. 348–380.

Blaug, Mark. "Economic Imperialism Revisited," *Yale Review*, Vol. 50, No. 3 (Spring 1961), pp. 335–349.

Borisov, Yu. V., Gromyko, A. A., and Israelian, V. L., eds. *Diplomatiya Sovremennogo Imperializma: Lyudi, Problemy, Metody*. Moscow, International Relations Publishing House, 1969.

71

Bosch, Juan. *Pentagonism: A Substitute for Imperialism*, tr. Helen R. Lane. New York: Grove Press, 1968.

Bukharin, Nikolai. *Imperialism and World Economy*. New York: Howard Fertig, 1966.

Churchward, L. G. "Towards the Understanding of Lenin's Imperialism," *Australian Journal of Politics and History*, Vol. V, No. 1 (May 1959).

Cohn-Bendit, Daniel, and Cohn-Bendit, Gabriel. *Obsolete Communism, The Left Wing Alternative*, tr. Arnold Pomerans. London: André Deutsch, 1968.

Crozier, Brian. *Neo-Colonialism*. London: Bodley Head, 1964.

de Beauvoir, Simone. *The Mandarins*. Cleveland, Meridian, 1960.

de Riencourt, Amaury. *The American Empire*. New York: Delta, 1970.

Domhoff, G. William. *Who Rules America?* Englewood Cliffs, N.J.: Prentice-Hall (Spectrum), 1967.

——. *The Higher Circles: The Governing Class in America*. New York: Random House, 1970.

——, and Ballard, Hoyt B., eds. *C. Wright Mills and the Power Elite*. Boston: Beacon, 1968.

Fann, K. T., and Hodges, Donald E., eds. *Readings in U.S. Imperialism*. Boston: Porter Sargent, 1971.

Fanon, Frantz. *The Wretched of the Earth*, tr. Constance Farrington. New York: Grove Press, 1966.

Fieldhouse, D. K., ed. *The Theory of Capitalist Imperialism*. London and Harlow: Longmans, Green, 1967.

Galbraith, John Kenneth. *The Affluent Society*. 2nd ed. rev. Boston: Houghton Mifflin, 1969. Originally published 1958.

——. *The New Industrial State*. New York: Signet, 1968.

Galtung, Johan. "A Structural Theory of Imperialism," *Journal of Peace Research*, Vol. 8, No. 2 (1971), pp. 81–117.

Gati, Charles. "Another Grand Debate? The Limitationist Critique of American Foreign Policy," *World Politics*, Vol. XXI, No. 1. (October 1968), pp. 133–151.

Gerassi, John, ed. *Venceremos! The Speeches and Writings of Ernesto Che Guevara.* New York: Simon and Schuster (Clarion Book), 1968.

Gordimer, Nadine. *A Guest of Honor.* New York: Viking, 1970.

Greene, Felix. *The Enemy: What Every American Should Know About Imperialism.* New York: Vintage, 1971.

Greene, Murray. "Schumpeter's Imperialism—A Critical Note," *Social Research,* Vol. 19, No. 4 (December 1952), pp. 453–463.

Harris, Nigel, and Palmer, John, eds. *World Crisis, Essays in Revolutionary Socialism.* London: Hutchinson, 1971.

Hayter, Teresa. *Aid as Imperialism.* Harmondsworth, Middlesex, England: Penguin, 1971.

Heimann, Eduard. "Schumpeter and the Problems of Imperialism," *Social Research,* Vol. 19, No. 2 (June 1952), pp. 177–197.

Hilferding, Rudolf. *Das Finanzkapital. Eine Studie über die jüngste Entwicklung des Kapitalismus.* Wien: Verlag der Wiener Volksbuchhandlung, 1920.

Hobson, J. A. *Imperialism, A Study.* London: Allen & Unwin, 1948. First published in 1902.

Hoffman, Stanley. *Gulliver's Troubles, or the Setting of American Foreign Policy.* Published for the Council on Foreign Relations. New York: McGraw-Hill, 1968.

——. "Weighing the Balance of Power," *Foreign Affairs,* Vol. 50, No. 4 (July 1972), pp. 618–643.

Horowitz, David, ed. *Containment and Revolution* (preface by Bertrand Russell). Boston: Beacon, 1967.

——, ed. *Corporations and the Cold War.* New York and London: Monthly Review Press, 1969.

Hovde, Brynjolf J. "Socialistic Theories of Imperialism Prior to the Great War," *Journal of Political Economy,* Vol. 36, No. 5 (October 1928), pp. 569–591.

Howe, Irving, ed. *A Dissenter's Guide to Foreign Policy.* Garden City, N.Y.: Anchor, 1968.

Jeffries, P. "New Trends in Imperialism," *Labour Review*, Vol. VII, No. 3 (1962).

Kautsky, John H. "J. A. Schumpeter and Karl Kautsky: Parallel Theories of Imperialism," *Midwest Journal of Political Science*, Vol. V, No. 2. (May 1961), pp. 101–128.

Kemp, Tom. *Theories of Imperialism*. London: Dobson, 1967.

——. "The Course of Capitalist Development," *Labour Review*, Vol. VI, No. 2 (1961).

——. "What Is Imperialism?," *Labour Review*, Vol. VII, No. 3 (1962).

Knorr, Klaus. "Theories of Imperialism," *World Politics*, Vol. IV., No. 3 (April 1952), pp. 402–431.

Koebner, Richard. *Empire*. New York: Grosset and Dunlap, The Universal Library, 1965.

——. "The Concept of Economic Imperialism," *Economic History Review*, Vol. II, ii, No. 1 (1949), pp. 1–29.

——. "The Emergence of the Concept of Imperialism," *Cambridge Journal*, Vol. V, No. 12 (September 1952).

——, and Schmidt, Helmut Dan. *Imperialism, The Story and Significance of a Political Word, 1840–1960*. Cambridge: Cambridge University Press, 1964.

Kolko, Gabriel. *The Roots of American Foreign Policy*. Boston: Beacon, 1969.

LaFeber, Walter. *The New Empire, An Interpretation of American Expansionism 1860–1898*. Ithaca, N.Y.: Cornell University Press, 1963.

Laing, R. D. *The Politics of Experience*. New York: Ballantine Books, 1967.

Landes, David S. "Some Thoughts on the Nature of Economic Imperialism," *Journal of Economic History*, Vol. 21, No. 4 (December 1961), pp. 496–512.

Langer, William L. "A Critique of Imperialism," *Foreign Affairs*, Vol. XIV (October 1935), pp. 102–119.

——. *The Diplomacy of Imperialism, 1890–1902*, 2nd ed. New York: Knopf, 1951.

Lenin, V. I. *Collected Works*, Vol. 39, "Notebooks on Imperialism," tr. Clemens Dutt. Moscow: Progress Publishers, 1968; London: Lawrence and Wishart.

——. *Imperialism, The Highest Stage of Capitalism*. New York: International Publishers, 1939.

——. *Lenin on the United States*. New York: International Publishers, 1970.

Lichtheim, George. *Imperialism*. New York and Washington: Praeger, 1971. See also Arnold, G. L.

Liska, George. *Imperial America, The International Politics of Primacy*. Baltimore: Johns Hopkins Press, 1967.

——. *Alliances and the Third World*. Baltimore: Johns Hopkins Press, 1968.

——. *War and Order: Reflections on Vietnam and History*. Baltimore: Johns Hopkins Press, 1968.

Luxemburg, Rosa. *The Accumulation of Capital*, tr. Agnes Schwarzschild. New York: Monthly Review Press, 1968.

Magdoff, Harry. *The Age of Imperialism*. New York and London: Monthly Review Press, 1969.

Mandel, Ernest. *Marxist Economic Theory*, tr. Brian Pearce. 2 vols. New York and London: Monthly Review Press, 1968.

——. *Europe versus America? Contradictions of Imperialism*, tr. Martin Rossdale. London: NLB, 1970.

Mannoni, O. *Prospero and Caliban, The Psychology of Colonization*, tr. Pamela Powesland. 2nd ed. New York: Praeger, 1956.

Marcuse, Herbert. *One-Dimensional Man*. Boston: Beacon, 1964.

May, Ernest R. *American Imperialism: A Speculative Essay*. New York: Atheneum, 1968.

Melman, Seymour. *Pentagon Capitalism—The Political Economy of War*. New York: McGraw-Hill, 1970.

Memmi, Albert. *The Colonizer and the Colonized*, tr. Howard Greenfield. Boston: Beacon, 1967. First published in French, 1957.

Mills, C. Wright. *The Power Elite*. New York: Oxford University Press, 1956.

Moon, Parker Thomas. *Imperialism and World Politics*. New York: Macmillan, 1926.

Morgenthau, Hans J. *A New Foreign Policy for the United States*. Published for the Council on Foreign Relations. New York: Praeger, 1969.

Morris, Bernard S. *International Communism and American Policy*. New York: Atherton, 1966.

Nadel, George H., and Curtis, Perry, eds. *Imperialism and Colonialism*. New York: Macmillan, 1964.

Neisser, Hans. "Economic Imperialism Reconsidered," *Social Research*, Vol. 27, No. 1 (Spring 1960), pp. 63–82.

Nettl, Peter. *Rosa Luxemburg*. 2 vols. London: Oxford University Press, 1966.

Nkrumah, Kwame. *Neo-Colonialism, The Last Stage of Imperialism*. New York: International Publishers, 1969.

Nobile, Philip, ed. *The Con III Controversy*. New York: Pocket Books, 1971.

O'Brien, Conor Cruise. "Contemporary Forms of Imperialism," *Studies on the Left*, Vol. 5, No. 4, 1965, pp. 13–26.

Oglesby, Carl, and Richard Shaull. *Containment and Change*. New York: Macmillan, 1967.

Pachter, Henry. "The Problem of Imperialism," *Dissent*, September–October 1970, pp. 461–488.

Paloczi-Horvath, George. *Youth Up In Arms*, A Political and Social World Survey 1955–1970. London: Weidenfeld and Nicolson, 1971.

The Pentagon Papers. New York: Bantam Books, 1971.

Reich, Charles A. *The Greening of America*. New York: Random House, 1970.

Rhodes, Robert I., ed. *Imperialism and Underdevelopment: A Reader*. New York and London: Monthly Review Press, 1970.

Rosenau, James N., ed. *Linkage Politics, Essay on the Conver-*

gence of National and International Systems. New York: Free Press, 1969.

Russett, Bruce M. *What Price Vigilance? The Burdens of National Defense.* New Haven: Yale University Press, 1970.

Said, Abdul A., ed. *America's World Role in the 70's.* Englewood Cliffs, N.J.: Prentice-Hall, Inc. (Spectrum), 1970.

Schumpeter, Joseph. *Imperialism and Social Classes.* New York: Meridian Books, 1955. Originally published in 1919.

Schurmann, Franz. "On Imperialism"—Essay I. July 31, 1967, 64 pages. No publisher.

Semmel, Bernard. *Imperialism and Social Reform: English Social-Imperial Thought 1895–1914.* Garden City, N.Y.: Anchor, 1968. First published by Allen and Unwin, 1960.

Servan-Schreiber, J. J. *The American Challenge,* tr. Ronald Steel. New York: Avon, 1969.

Slater, Philip. *The Pursuit of Loneliness, American Culture at the Breaking Point.* Boston: Beacon, 1970.

Snyder, Louis L. *The Imperialism Reader: Documents and Readings on Modern Expansionism.* Princeton, N.J.: Van Nostrand, 1962.

Steel, Ronald. *Pax Americana.* New York: Viking, 1967.

——. *A Chronicle of the American Empire.* New York: Random House, 1971.

Sternberg, Fritz. *Capitalism and Socialism on Trial,* tr. Edward Fitzgerald. New York: John Day, 1950.

Stretton, Hugh. *The Political Sciences.* London: Routledge and Kegan Paul, 1969.

Sweezy, Paul M. *The Theory of Capitalist Development.* New York: Monthly Review Press, 1968. First published in 1942.

Teodori, Massimo, ed. *The New Left: A Documentary History.* Indianapolis and New York: Bobbs-Merrill, 1969.

Thornton, A. P. *Doctrines of Imperialism.* New York: John Wiley and Sons, 1965.

———. *The Imperial Idea and Its Enemies, A Study in British Power*. Garden City, N.Y.: Anchor, 1968.

———. "Colonialism," *International Journal*, Vol. 17, No. 4 (Autumn 1962), pp. 335–357.

Triska, Jan F., and Finley, David D. *Soviet Foreign Policy*. New York: Macmillan, 1968.

Tucker, Robert W. *Nation or Empire? The Debate Over American Foreign Policy*. Baltimore: Johns Hopkins Press, 1968.

———. *The Radical Left and American Foreign Policy*. Baltimore: Johns Hopkins Press, 1971.

Varga, E., and Mendelsohn, L. *New Data for Lenin's "Imperialism."* New York: International Publishers, 1940.

Veblen, Thorstein. *The Vested Interests and the Common Man*. New York: Capricorn Books, 1969.

Welch, William. *American Images of Soviet Foreign Policy*. New Haven: Yale University Press, 1970.

Wesson, Robert G. *The Imperial Order*. Berkeley and Los Angeles: University of California Press, 1967.

Williams, William Appleman. *The Tragedy of American Diplomacy*, rev. ed. New York: Delta, 1962.

Winslow, E. M. *The Pattern of Imperialism: A Study in the Theories of Power*. New York: Columbia University Press, 1948.

Woddis, Jack. *An Introduction to Neo-Colonialism*. New York: International Publishers, 1967.

Wright, Harrison, M. "Imperialism: The Word and Its Meaning," *Social Research*, Vol. 34, No. 4 (Winter 1967), pp. 660–674.

Index

American foreign policy: imperialism of, 4–7, 34–39; linkage with domestic policy, 8–9; economic influences on, 23–24, 35–39, 50–51, 57; and class structure, 34–35; neo-realist theory of, 40–52; American people's influence on, 50–51; political influence on, 57–58; critics of, 61–64

balance of power strategy, 62–63
Baran, Paul A., 2, 12
Beauvoir, Simone de, ix
Bernstein, Eduard, 20, 53
Bukharin, Nikolai, 16n

capitalism: Lenin's theories on, 12–17; unisystem of, 32–33; as influencing U.S. foreign policy, 35–38; Marxist-Leninist theories as now invalid, 54–57; in advanced vs. underdeveloped countries, 54–55
change: and consciousness, 9–10, 70; how to bring about?, 64–66
China, changing U.S. policy on, 50
class structure, American, 34–35
Cohn-Bendit, D. and G., 3
colonialism: and Lenin's theory of imperialism, 17–18; and newly independent states, 27–32; neocolonialism, 27–32
Communist International, 21
Communist League, 21
Communist Manifesto, 31
consciousness: and radical change, 9–10; new political, 68–70

counter-culture, 9–10, 68–69
critics of American foreign policy, 61–64

Domhoff, G. William, 34

East-Central Europe, Soviet policy in, 5
economic influences on foreign policy, 23–24, 35–39, 50–51, 57
European stability, 46

foreign policy: imperialism of, 4, 6–7, 34–39; linkage with domestic policy, 8–9; and economic policy, 23–24, 35–39, 50–51, 57; neo-realist theory of, 40–52; of socialist governments, 55–56
"free" society, 66–67

Gati, Charles, 6
Great Powers theory, 8, 57–58
Greening of America, The, 68, 70

Hilferding, Rudolf, 12
Hobson, J. A., 12, 20, 61–62
Hoffman, Stanley, 62–63
Humphrey, Hubert H., 62, 64

Imperial America: The International Politics of Primacy, 41, 51
imperialism: why reexamine theories of?, vii–x, 10–11; Marxist-Leninist theory of, vii–ix, 12–39; difference between Soviet and capitalist, 4–6; of U.S. foreign policy, 6–7; meaning of

79